T0162417

The Vél d'Hiv Raid
The French Police
at the Service of the Gestapo

THE VÉL D'HIV RAID
The French Police
at the Service of the Gestapo

Maurice Rajsfus

Translated by Levi Laub
Foreword by Michel Warschawski

DoppelHouse Press • Los Angeles

The Vél d'Hiv Raid:
The French Police at the Service of the Gestapo
By Maurice Rajsfus
Translated by Levi Laub
Foreword by Michel Warschawski

DoppelHouse Press © 2017

PRINTED IN THE UNITED STATES

Publisher's Cataloging-in-Publication data

Names: Rajsfus, Maurice, 1928-, author. | Laub, Levi, translator. |
Warschawski, Michel, foreword author.
Title: The Vél d'Hiv raid : the French police at the service of the
Gestapo / by Maurice Rajsfus ; translated by Levi Laub ; with a
foreword by Michel Warschawski.
Description: Includes bibliographical references. | Los Angeles, CA:
Dopplehouse Press, 2017.
Identifiers: ISBN 978-0-9978184-5-1 (Hardcover) | 978-0-9978184-6-8
(pbk.) | 978-0-9978184-9-2 (ebook) | LCCN 2017946124
Subjects: Police--France--History--20th century. | France--History--
German occupation, 1940–1945. | Vichy (France)--Politics and
government. | Jews--Persecutions--France. | Holocaust, Jewish (1939–
1945)--France--Personal narratives. | France--Ethnic relations. |
France--History--German occupation, 1940–1945. | BISAC HISTORY /
Holocaust | HISTORY / Europe / France | HISTORY / Jewish
Classification: LCC D802.F8 R285 2017 | DDC 363.2/0944--dc23

DoppelHouse Presss
Los Angeles, California

CONTENTS

FOREWORD TO THE ENGLISH EDITION

By Michel Warschawski

THE PUBLICATION IN ENGLISH of Maurice Rajsfus' book on the Vél d'Hiv Raid is right on time. Originally published fifteen years ago[1] the book made known to a new generation one of the most sordid chapters in the history of the French State and its collaboration with the Nazi occupiers. The author relates the story of the Vél d'Hiv Raid in a hundred extremely well documented pages, describing how 13,152 men, women, children and old people were delivered by the French gendarmes to the Gestapo, to be imprisoned at the winter sporting stadium in Paris, the Vélodrome d'Hiver, and then in the detention camp at Drancy, before being sent to the death camps in Eastern Europe.

But Maurice Rajsfus is not only a historian of the raid: he lived it in his flesh, saw it with his own eyes, and if he had not had the audacity and ingenuity of a Parisian street urchin, son of immigrant Polish Jews that he was, he would have suffered the same fate as his parents, deported and assassinated in Auschwitz.

---

[1] Maurice Rajsfus, *La Rafle du Vél d'Hiv*, Presses Universitaires de France, 2002. The book was part of the popular series "Que sais-je?"

Without making improper comparisons, the roundup of the Vél d'Hiv is a very current topic. Maurice Rajsfus' narrative can help us grasp both the logic and the implications of a policy of exclusion of communities because of their ethnic, national or religious origin, resulting that they are not protected by the State of which they are a part. Indeed, since that time, these policies of exclusion practiced by States defining themselves as democratic have not led yet to mass massacres, as was the case under the Vichy regime. But that fact cannot justify the silence and indifference of the average citizen who can see discrimination as it happens.

Whether Roma or other communities lacking the right color or accent, or immigrants fleeing war or hunger, in democratic Europe millions of men and women are victims of exclusion, repression, and racist acts, which are committed by state institutions, fascist parties, and too often ordinary citizens. Xenophobia is steadily growing and racism is becoming more uninhibited. For the first time since the victory over Nazism, racist and xenophobic views can be expressed popularly without disguise, far beyond the utterances and movements of the extreme right.

Both in the States and in Europe the policies leading to roundups and deportation have historically been practiced with mechanisms strangely similar to the Vél d'Hiv Raid. First the identification of "the other," then its stigmatization, then the social exclusion followed by the expulsion from the national body and at the same time, a gradual rise in popular violence and state violence, which can go as far as massacre. This is no more clearly illustrated in the United States than in the fate of the American Indian.

The Vél d'Hiv Raid is an emblematic moment specifically in the policy of racist discrimination against Jews (and others) in Vichy France, which led tens of thousands of them to extermination camps. In order to be effective, this policy required the collaboration of several actors: first, the Nazis and the German occupation forces, who put this policy in place and directed it. Then the collaboration of the Vichy regime, with its politicians, gendarmes and fascist militias. Often they were overzealous and—as Maurice Rajsfus reminds us in his book—they expanded the roundup of foreign-born Jews to children of French nationality who were not included in the original German orders. Without the active assistance of the French administration and the French police, the Vél d'Hiv Raid, and later on the deportation of more than 75,000 Jews from France, could not have been done so effectively.

And then there is a third actor, to whom Maurice Rajsfus had previously devoted two other books: the notables of the Jewish community of France, organized in the UGIF (Union générale des israélites de France). This latter played a role similar to that of the Jewish Councils (Judenrat) in the ghettos of Eastern Europe. This foreword is not the appropriate place to evaluate the choices open to the community leaders, nor the responsibilities of each of them. While Maurice has been able to make a convincing case regarding the UGIF's collaboration, the responsibilities of the individuals concerned require more nuances. There was a mix of the corrupt, self-seeking calculators, cowards and naifs who believed in saving one group of Jews by sacrificing another—in particular the so-called foreigners—as well as true resistors who knew how to use their position to save the greatest number possible.

Maurice Rajsfus' research on the UGIF is in line with that of other historians of the Jewish Councils in Poland and leads to the same conclusion: the official institutions of the Jewish communities facilitated the policy of exclusion which led to extermination.

The deportation of 75,000 Jews of France, including the more than 13,000 rounded up in the Vélodrome d'Hiver, can and must open our eyes to the contemporary mechanisms of racist exclusion. How can we ever forget the roundups of Algerians during the war of national liberation and the massacre that followed on October 17, 1961? How can we fail to make the connection to Donald Trump's policy towards Mexican and Central American refugees? The clown of the White House is not a laughing matter: we do not forget that our parents' generation was replete with jokes about another clown who shouted obscenities at Munich and Nuremberg, before they realized that a bloody monster was hiding behind this pathetic character who, during the thirteen years to come, would provoke the deaths of tens of millions of human beings.

In telling us the story of the Vél d'Hiv Raid, Maurice does not speak of the numerous acts of solidarity on the part of non-Jewish French towards their neighbors, friends, or even ordinary passers-by. Certainly, the great majority of French society collaborated in the deportation of the Jews of France, or at least closed its eyes. Despite the claims of General de Gaulle, France was not a "resisting country," and the resistors were a small minority... until the moment the Allied forces liberated France from the Nazi occupation, the moment when hundreds of thousands of men and women rewrote the story of their lives during the previous five years. That said, there were thousands of good people who did things, big or small, to try to assist the persecuted Jews. Including during the Vél d'Hiv Raid.

My mother lived through the entire Nazi occupation in Paris, as a young student of Khâgne [literature and humanities] at the Lycée Fenelon, wearing the yellow star and subject to all the discriminations of which the Jews were victims, including the most "French" amongst them. Being of old French stock, Alsatian in fact, she and her family were not picked up in the Vél d'Hiv Raid. Throughout her years as mother and grandmother, but also her work as an educator, she never ceased to relay what she considered the most important lesson of her experience during the war— not the will for revenge, nor any claim to the "uniqueness of Jewish destiny," but the importance of solidarity. "If we are alive, your grandparents, your aunt, and me—it is thanks to solidarity. My school friends at Fenelon, our concierge, your grandfather's colleagues at the SNCF [the national railroad service, where he worked throughout the war at the Gare de l'Est, with the yellow star on his jacket, and never missed the Saturday prayers at the Cadet street synagogue, thanks to his fellow workers who covered for him]—it's thanks to them and their solidarity that we were able to escape deportation."

In the United States too, spontaneous as well as

organized protests have dramatically countered previous indifference to the policies of exclusion and ostracism. Tens of thousands of protesters have clogged the roads and shut down major airports demanding that hastily imposed immigrant travel bans be lifted and discrimination towards Muslim refugees and visitors be dropped immediately. As Walter Benjamin taught us so insightfully, the suffering of our elders can be the best incitement to do good, and to make true the ubiquitous and often misused slogan "never again."

– Jerusalem, February 2017

1

THE UNVARNISHED TRUTH

THE GREAT RAID of July 16 and 17, 1942—known as the Vél d'Hiv Raid—was neither the first nor the last of the racial operations conducted by the French police. Nonetheless it was the most significant and symbolic of those repressive actions. First because of the number of people arrested—13,512,— then because, for the first time, women and children were targets of the raid, and finally because the Vélodrome d'Hiver itself left such a mark on people's memory.

From May 14, 1941, to the end of spring 1944 there were numerous raids, but they did not have the same impact. The Drancy camp, which would "welcome" many of those arrested on July 16, 1942, became the definitive symbol of the French concentration camp during the era of the Nazi occupation. This genuine eyesore, located in the heart of a city, would not allow one to forget that about fifty of these detention centers blanketed the country—principally in the so-called "free" zone.

The great raid, conducted entirely by the French police, left an indelible mark. Above all, it was a demonstration of the malignant power of a corps of government servants that had lost its bearings. Recalling that event should serve to alert citizens of a free country about the abuses of strong governments.

It is worth remembering that an old xenophobic tradition would ease the way to casting out the foreigners who had supposedly come to batten on the French. Since the end of the nineteenth century, hunting down Italians in the southeast of France and Belgians in the north, had created a malignant atmosphere. It is only a small step from rejection to wanting to lock someone up. So it bears remembering that since 1927, the internment of foreigners in concentration camps during times of war—or their expulsion—had been proposed by men in power in Republican France. It was quasi officially that, in a publication prefaced by Édouard Heriot, *France and foreigners,* Charles Lambert, deputy and high commissioner for immigration and nationalization, already invoked the "Invasion of the foreigners." There was a desire to distinguish between good and bad foreigners, those who could be assimilated and the others who rebelled against it, for whom there was envisaged the creation of "irredentist centers."

In unison with the great Republicans who devoted themselves to xenophobia, the militant extreme-right chimed in with its own contribution—sworn hatred. Thus, the writer Henri Béraud did not hesitate to demonize "the great torrent of Neapolitan scum, the Levantine hordes in rags, the sad stinking Slavs, the dreadful Andalusian poor, the Judean streetwalkers"[1] who, in his eyes, dishonored France. The path was cleared for the xenophobic and anti-Semitic factions who would demand without hesitation that the country be cleared of elements considered "dangerous." Can one not recall that since 1937, Louis Darquier, aka Pellepoix, was already putting the finishing touches on a Statute governing the Jews of France?

The Daladier law decrees of May 2 and 14, 1938, re-enforced on November 12 of that same year, already specified the threats hanging over the immigrant workers that the Minister of the Interior, Albert Sarraut, had characterized as the "foreign hoi polloi" that the France of The Rights of Man must push out.

The house arrests foreseen in this battery of decrees against foreigners whose legal status was irregular, would be transformed into internment under harsh conditions when the remnants of the Spanish Republican armies came flooding over the Pyrenees after February 1939. Tens of thousands of them would inaugurate the first French concentration camps. A significant bibliography retraces the conditions of confinement of these Spanish combatants whose only crime was to oppose Franco's coup. The French gendarmes treated them like criminals.[2]

Thus, the country's concentration camp system was initiated. The carrying out of raids was still to come. That would happen after the month of October 1939, when

---

1 Henri Béraud in *Gringoire,* May 1936.
2 Louis Stein, *Between Death and Exile: The Spanish Republicans in France,* 1939–1955, Harvard University Press, 1980.

Albert Sarraut, still Minister of Foreign Affairs, decided to imprison German nationals residing in France. They were mostly anti-fascists, refugees in our country, and German Jews fleeing racial persecution. (The Nazis had already left France.) The house arrests would facilitate the capture of several thousands of those Germans (subsequently extended to Austrians, Czechs and a few hundred of "undetermined" nationality). Here as well, a number of works describe the treatment reserved for these anti-Fascists—and these democrats—opposed to the Nazi Germany that France was supposed to be fighting. A second wave of arrests would sweep over the German immigrants in May 1940.[3]

These Germans would soon be turned over to the Nazis under Article 19 of the Armistice Convention of June 22, 1940.[4] It marked the end of an episode the American historians, Marrus and Paxton, would call "Vichy before Vichy."

---

3 Two works in particular call attention to this inglorious episode: *The Scum of the Earth,* by Arthur Koestler (Macmillan, 1941), and *The Devil in France,* by Lion Feuchtwanger (Hutchinson, 1950).

4 "… The French government must hand over, upon request, all German nationals designated by the government of the Reich, who are to be found in France…"

2

PRELUDES TO THE GREAT RAID:
The Preparations of the Vichy Government

LONG BEFORE NAZI GERMANY, which occupied three fifths of France, would impose its rule over the government of the free zone, Pétain and his ministers were already busy cracking down on foreigners, "the cause of the country's misfortunes," and most directly, the Jews.

It is too simplistic to explain the racial persecution carried out in France from 1940 to 1944 solely in terms of the Nazis' desire to eliminate the Jews. As in all the countries of occupied Europe, it was necessary for them to find allies if not accomplices in their labor of destruction. Thus, in France, in Belgium and in the Netherlands, xenophobes and hard-bitten racists gave their support to the extermination, just as in Poland, in Byelorussia and in the Ukraine. Without that support, in the case of France, as the SS General Oberg testified, the slaughter of the Jews, but also the communists, the Gaullists and the Freemasons, could never have achieved such devastating results.

The predicament of foreigners, already hardly enviable at the time of the defeat, became alarming with the first decrees enacted by the Vichy government. Of course the most vicious xenophobes of the 1930s were in the government or the corridors of power.

Beginning on July 27, 1940, a Commission created at Vichy was charged with reviewing naturalizations effected after August 10, 1927.[1] On August 16 a law regulating the medical profession was meant to prepare the public for the expulsion of Jewish practitioners. On August 27, the Marchandeau law of April 21, 1939, which banned racial defamation, was repealed. On September 10, 1940, a law, regulating access to the bar, targeted Jewish lawyers. Finally, on September 27, the Vichy government promulgated a law regarding the "surplus of foreigners in the French economy." This allowed the rapid internment—in the unoccupied zone— of 40,000 foreigners, assembled in GTEs, [*Groupements de travailleurs étrangers*—Foreign workers' groups] under the formal authority of the Ministry of Labor but effectively under the supervision of the gendarmerie. Jewish internees in the camps were grouped in companies called "Palestinian."

This series of laws precedes or accompanies the promulgation of the first German edict summoning Jews in the occupied zone to register themselves at police stations or substations. This same law goes on to define Jews according to the Nuremberg racial laws.[2]

On October 3, 1940, the first Statute of the Jews of

---

1 For more about this legislation, already stamped with racism and active xenophobia, one should consult the work of Dominique Rémy, *Les lois de Vichy,* Romillet, 1992.

2 Adopted by the September 15, 1935 Congress of the Nazi Party, the Nuremberg laws excluded Jews from the national community based on religious criteria.

France is enacted according to criteria more drastic than those of the Nazis, with Jews being defined according to race and no longer by religion alone. The new Vichy law of October 4th specified that "foreign nationals of the Jewish religion, as of the date of the promulgation of the present law, could be interned in special camps by decision of the prefect of the département of their residence." On October 7th, the Crémieux law dating back to October 24, 1870, was repealed. It had bestowed French nationality on the Jews of Algeria. Henceforth they would be treated according to the laws governing the indigenous population.

This gradual preparation would accelerate with the creation of a Jewish data file at the police headquarters in Paris and the occupied zone, and with the application of the Jewish Statute, the exclusion of Jews from commercial and industrial professions as well as the civil service. Other repressive measures were prepared and on March 29, 1941, the Vichy government presided over the formation of the General Commission for Jewish Affairs. The main purpose of this body was the "Aryanization" of commerce and industry in liaison with the police. Xavier Vallat, the first head of this agency was already well known for his violently anti-Semitic sentiments.

At this point the pace of the big operations began to speed up, although apparently only foreign Jews were hunted down at first. Thus, on May 14, 1941, approximately 6,000 Jewish foreigners living in Paris were invited by their neighborhood police chiefs to appear at their local police station for "a review of their situation." The "review" locations included the Japy gymnasium, the Tourelles and the Napoleon barracks, and the Opera. About 3,800 showed up and were escorted by the gendarmes to two internment camps in the Loiret: Pithiviers and Beaune-la-Rolande.[3] Two documents issued by police headquarters dated May 14, 1942, convey the tone and witness the willingness of the Paris police to respect the orders of the Occupier.

> In accord with the General Commission of the French government in the occupied territories, and at the request of the Occupation Authorities, police headquarters proceeded this morning, by summons, to round up Polish Nationals, Jews, aged 18 to 40, Czech nationals and former Austrians, aged 18 to 60. Of the 6,494 that were summoned, 3,747 were conveyed by four special trains to the camps of Pithiviers and Beaune-la-Rolande (Loiret). Those who, having been summoned, failed to show up at the roundup centers, will be subject to further searches. These operations did not give rise to any incidents.[4]

The other document was issued by the General Intelligence Service, which in those uncertain times, continued to judge the political climate and the behavior of citizens throughout the country.

_____

3 There is only one book about this first wave of arrests: *Le Billet Vert,* by David Diamant, Le Renouveau, 1977.
4 Archive of the Prefecture of Police, APP, series 1817, B 51.

The internment measure undertaken today against the Jews provoked a general panic in the Israelite circles of the capital. Some claimed to know that they would be taken to factories in Germany, others that they would be deported to Africa. The Jews seem to be distressed by the indifference on the part of the French regarding these internments. Particularly, they stated that similar measures had been carried out in Belgium but they were revoked due to the discontent that they caused in the general population.

Among the newspapers that enthusiastically reported this seemingly legal (since it was carried out by the French police) raid, one deserves mention, as it offered its readers an account dripping with hatred. This attack is related here with all the coarse vulgarity that the collaborationist press is capable of, believing as it did that the French police were never sufficiently repressive.

For the last two days the Paris ghetto has been in turmoil. The day before yesterday, many Jewish foreigners received a summons at their homes asking them to come to a specified place at 7 a.m. the following morning for "a matter that concerns them." The note added: "Please come accompanied by a member of your family." Thus at 7 a.m. yesterday a few thousand Israelites showed up at the sites they had been ordered to go to: The Japy gymnasium, the Minimes barracks,

Grange-aux-Balles street or Édouard-Paillerons street.[5] Some joked, some scoffed, but the laughter became forced when it was announced: "We are going to give the persons accompanying their relative a sheet which they should read carefully. They have three quarters of an hour to make the prescribed little trip and bring back the requested objects." The sheet read: "You must go immediately to your relative's home and bring them back a blanket, a change of underwear, some place settings, a plate and provisions for twenty four hours, etc.[6]

The *Paris-Midi* journalist could not hide his satisfaction upon seeing this wave of arrests carried out. He continued with a vengeful pen:

All of a sudden, everyone understood. It was at last the realization of the law of October 4, 1940. Less than one hour later the relatives reappeared with the little bundle that had been hastily tied together... Some hysterical outbursts, some noisy demonstrations, and then everything came back to order. Between rows of police and republican guards, the Jews got into buses and police vans. By 5 p.m. they were on the platforms of the Gare d'Austerlitz.

---

5 The summons cited here also contained this threat: "A person who does not show up on the date and hour specified will be subject to the most severe sanctions."
6 *Paris-Midi,* May 15, 1941.

Five thousand Jews departed. Five thousand Jewish
foreigners slept their first night in a concentration camp.
Five thousand fewer parasites in Greater Paris, which
had contracted a fatal disease. The first extraction is
accomplished. Others will follow."[7]

Not to be outdone, *Paris-Soir* appears with an equally
hateful front-page story, titled: "France is freed of the yoke of
Israel." Parisians would read,

Today, the French government, in accord with the
law of October 4, carried out the first measure against
the Jews. Under orders from Vichy, this morning the
police summoned to designated centers, some 5,000
Jews, chosen among the foreigners, particularly Polish,
Czechs, and some Austrians; men between the ages of 18
to 40.[8]

The following day, some of the headlines on the first
page of *Paris-Soir* were devoted to an appeal to pursue the
racial persecution: "The purification of Paris has begun,"
then "Israel must be finished off!" and, finally, a great classic:
"Jews are not to be tolerated in society except in homeopathic
doses, Mr. Xavier Vallat tells us."[9]

Police headquarters, organizer of this raid by summons,
did a good job. An important "welcoming committee" kept

_____

7 Ibid.
8 *Paris-Soir,* May 15, 1941.
9 *Paris-Soir,* May 16, 1941.

careful watch over the arrest operations, ready to deal with any contingency. "As soon as the first arrivals appeared at the centers, they were penned in behind heavy rope barriers. They were lined up in alphabetical order."[10] No details were overlooked by the vigilant police. Confronted with a mass of worried, paralyzed foreigners, suddenly transformed into prisoners, the police behaved roughly, the guardians of public order not being content with merely carrying out their orders. "They were packed into the buses, the police carried on brutally while Gestapo agents stayed discreetly off to the side."[11] As if that was not enough, headquarters was careful to warn the regular passengers rushing to get to their trains. "At the Austerlitz station the trains had been specially prepared for their benefit. To avoid all contact between the captive Jews and other passengers each train displayed a yellow flag, a sign of contagious disease (cholera, plague)..."[12]

After the arrests of May 14—by summons—the German authorities, in collaboration with Vichy, decide to have the Paris police headquarters carry out a raid on a grand scale comprising the entire 11th arrondissement of Paris. For the Parisian Gestapo and the chief of its Department IV J, SS Théo Dannecker, this operation would serve as a test to gauge the determination of the officers as well as the rank and file police. This raid, which started at dawn on August 20, 1941, would go on for some days because the number of

_____

10 In *Le billet vert,* by David Diamant, op. cit., p. 27.
11 Ibid, p. 28.
12 Ibid.

Jews (French and foreigners this time) arrested was judged insufficient by the German police, which did not participate but was kept informed on an hourly basis as the operation unfolded. That's why the raid would be extended to other quartiers of Paris. By August 25, 4,230 arrests had been made. On the evening of August 20 the camp at Drancy was opened. Well known activist and Nazi hunter Serge Klarsfeld provides an interesting point of information: In contrast to the previous action, the heads of the German police went around the Vichy police chiefs and spoke directly to the Paris police headquarters, which had been selected as project manager for the raid.[13] What particularly displeased the Vichy Minister of the Interior was that native born French Jews were arrested as well, especially some "200 intellectuals," notably lawyers.

Though limited, this was a raid of considerable scope. From 5:30 in the morning the metro stations in the affected area (from Place de la République to Place de la Nation, and from Place de la Bastille to Père-Lachaise) were closed. According to an internal memo at the police headquarters, some 2,400 inspectors, officers and patrolmen were charged with making the arrests under the control of the German police.[14] Following the raid, according to a report by the General Intelligence Service, the reactions of the Parisian population are fairly constrained. Satisfaction and indifference are dominant but with one regret, namely that

---

13 In *Vichy-Auschwitz* by Serge Klarsfeld, Fayard, 1983, Vol. I, p. 25.
14 Ibid, pp. 27–28.

this measure equally affected French Jews, particularly, the veterans of two wars.

Superintendent Rottée, a high-ranking official at police headquarters, had a tight accounting for the progress of the operation:

– 8:30 a.m.:	600 arrests
– 9:15 a.m.:	2,000 arrests
– 2:00 p.m.:	2,900 arrests

This information, coming from the Intelligence Service, left him unsatisfied, and at 2:10 p.m., the Superintendent sent a hand-written memo to the different police departments: "The German police feel that there are insufficient arrests. Another 1,000 must be carried out before tomorrow evening."[15]

With little strokes, the racial persecution continued to develop. December 12, 1941, saw the only raid carried out by the German police. About 450 *feldgendarmes* and members of the SIPO-SD,[16] assisted at times by the French police, arrested almost 750 French Jews classified as "notables."

Big maneuvers were conspicuous after the return of Pierre Laval as the head of the Vichy government and the accession of René Bousquet to the post of General Minister of the Police. A former member of Albert Sarraut's cabinet, as Minister of the Interior (where he dealt with the matter of

---

15 APP, series BA-1816 (Superintendent Rottée would be shot in December, 1944).

16 *Sicherheitspolizei* (Security Police) one of the branches of the Gestapo along with the SD – *Sicherheitsdienst* (Security Service).

foreigners), it seemed that Bousquet's first and only concern was to obtain complete freedom of action for the French police, within the scope, of course, of the priorities set by the Occupier.[17] Rapidly, the difficulties of communication between the French and German police administrations would be smoothed out. Bousquet would also take under his direct control the members of the national gendarmerie, the mobile guard squadrons and even the police force created by the Commission for Jewish Affairs.

During his trial, Karl Oberg, chief of the German police in Paris, let the cat out of the bag:

> It was in our interest to have the French police united
> under a single command... in accordance with the
> agreement I made with Bousquet, the French police
> acted independently—following common guidelines laid
> down by the German police and under the responsibility
> of Bousquet. This also applied to the Jewish Question.[18]

It became evident that, henceforth, under the supervision of the Gestapo, Bousquet would be able to carry out planned racial crackdowns and the great raid of July 16, 1942, was already contemplated.

Fortunately, numerous archives allow us to follow the preparation stages of the approaching grand-scale racial persecution. Those documents demonstrate the synergy

17 See the work of Pascale Froment, *René Bousquet,* Stock, Au vif du sujet, 1994, and *La Police de Vichy, les forces de l'ordre francaises au service de la Gestapo* by Maurice Rajsfus, Le Cherche Midi Éditeur, 1995.
18 In *Vichy-Auschwitz,* op. cit., p. 59.

that existed between the German and French police. Acting without the incitement of the Occupier, the Paris police had already established its own anti-Jewish departments. From the early days of January 1941, SS officials had offices at police headquarters. Mission: Facilitate an efficient liaison between the French police and Department IV J of the Gestapo, directed by Théo Dannecker. The hunt that began with the raids of May 14 and those of August 20 and 21, 1941, was facilitated by the census of October 1940, which permitted the creation of the Jewish data file at police headquarters, under the responsibility of André Tulard. This "tool" was so useful that it was characterized as a *Model file* by SS Dannecker. Colonel Knochen, chief of the Paris Gestapo, would later say: "The general Jewish File, which was the only means of locating the Jews, the number of children at a given place, all those details, would not have been known except thanks to the French police, who gave them to the *SIPO* in addition to the reports and numbers from French intelligence."[19]

It is well documented that there were many links between the two police forces even before the arrival of René Bousquet as Vichy police chief. This was confirmed once again in a report of February 22, 1942, signed by SS Dannecker: "The French police detectives, who trained for their work with our local Jewish affairs department, serve today as a sort of elite troop and as instructors for the new French recruits to the anti-Jewish police. In the occupied zone, the control of the anti-Jewish police by our local department of Jewish

19 Cited in *La grand rafle du Vél d'Hiv,* by Claude Lèvy and Paul Tillard, J'ai lu, 1967, p. 289.

affairs is assured."[20] In fact, at police headquarters, one department of the Intelligence Service, under the direction of chief detective Sadowski, was charged with preparation of efficient repressive operations—undoubtedly so as not to abandon the field to the Police for Jewish Affairs, who reported to the Jewish Question Commission.

On March 10, 1942, less than three weeks before the departure from Compiègne of the first deportation convoy, SS Dannecker, in Compiègne, raised the possibility of the deportation to the East of 5,000 Jews. The problem of rail transportation still needed to be resolved. That number would soon be revised upwards.

It is clear that one sector of public opinion, stirred up by the collaborationist press, expected repressive measures against the Jews. At the front of this pack, the daily *Au Pilori,* did not hide its impatience:

> I don't know what solution will be proposed for the
> Jewish problem after the war. But I know that we could
> address the problem without waiting, with a temporary
> solution that would re-establish some equity in an
> upside down France, where the national Revolution
> is still in the stages of formation. It would be enough
> to decide, purely and simply, that until the return of
> the last of our captives, a Jew cannot enjoy, under any
> pretext, a moral or material condition superior to that of

---

20 In *Vichy-Auschwitz,* op. cit., p. 195.

a French prisoner of war. Therefore, all Jewish adults, without exception, without preferential treatment, without any possible protection, should be in prison camps with armed guards. I repeat: it is not a matter of being cruel, or of seeking blind vengeance. It is a matter of justice and self-defense. It is also a matter of using a work force, although an inferior one to be sure, but abundant and at a good price, to carry out needed public works, clearing snow in the winter, helping farmers in the summer. Of course, if we carry out this project, which I don't hesitate to describe as full of moderation and humanity, Universal Conscience, so indifferent to the hardships of Aryans, will howl with rage. Need we say that we couldn't care less about Universal Conscience.[21]

21 Pierre-André Cousteau in *Je suis partout,* May 23, 1942.

3

THE PREPARATION FOR THE RAID

ON JANUARY 20, 1942, after the Wannsee conference, the *final solution* to the Jewish problem was set in motion, even though massacres were already the rule on the Russian front since June of 1941. The racial repression that was unfolding in the Paris region of France in 1941 represented simply a dress rehearsal. The course had been set. From Berlin, the Parisian departments of the Gestapo were informed that trains, in sufficient numbers, would be provided as soon as needed for the anticipated raids. It was clearly established that only the French police would move into action as soon as they received the orders.

On June 15, 1942, a total of 100,000 Jews were already targeted for deportation—including the unoccupied zone.

Another document from that same date, also signed by SS Dannecker, referred to the rapid formation of fifteen convoys of 1,000 Jews.[1]

On June 18, Dannecker was reassured: The trains needed for the deportations to come were definitely at his disposal. Already, he thought it "necessary to make

---

1 In *Vichy-Auschwitz*, op. cit., pp. 202–204.

known immediately, by telex, the chronological order for the departure stations."[2] The search for the temporary internment locations was given priority. For this purpose, the camps of Drancy, Pithiviers and Beaune-la-Rolande were partially emptied by the deportation convoys scheduled for June 22, 25 and 26.

Still, on June 18, it was René Bousquet who wanted to let General Oberg, supreme SS commander in France, know that his police awaited their orders.

> You know the French police. They undoubtedly
> have their flaws, but they also have their merits. I
> am convinced that, reorganized on a new basis, and
> forcefully led, they are capable of rendering great
> service. You have already seen their performance and
> the efficiency of their action in numerous matters. I am
> sure that they can do even better.[3]

The Gestapo departments had nothing to worry about. René Bousquet had become Minister General of the Vichy Police only two months ago but he was already prepared to carry out racial repression.

On June 22, 1942, from Berlin, Adolf Eichmann informed his Minister of Foreign Affairs about the progress of the raids project in France: "There is a plan to send to work, in the Auschwitz camp, a first contingent made up of

---

2 Archives of the Center for Contemporary Jewish Documentation, CDJC, XXV b-38.
3 In *Vichy-Auschwitz*, op. cit. p. 209.

some 40,000 Jews coming from the French occupied zone."[4] On June 26, SS Dannecker sent a memo to his superiors: "Bousquet is ready to send us, to start with, 10,000 Jews, at our disposal for evacuation to the East."[5] In the same text he provided details that leave no doubt about the cooperation between the French and German police. " I let Leguay[6] know that on June 29,1942, I expect to receive a concrete plan for the arrest of 22,000 Jews in the départements of the Seine and the Seine-et-Oise."[7]

On June 29, SS Dannecker spoke to the chiefs of the SIPO-SD in France to inform them of hesitations on the part of Prefect Leguay, who would prefer first to arrest the "truly undesirable elements," understood to mean foreign Jews. Dannecker, who did not like nuances, got right to the point:

I told Leguay that he needed to contact the chief of police in Paris, that henceforth, I probably would take control of this action, and for about two weeks, beginning on a certain date, I would need, for that purpose, at least 2,500 uniformed men of the French police, and furthermore, another contingent of the judicial police.[8]

The great raid is on the agenda. The actual work will be carried out by the French police as the occupation authorities

---

4 In *Vichy-Auschwitz,* op. cit. p. 214.

5 CDJC, XXVI-33.

6 René Bousquet's representative in the occupied zone.

7 CDJC, XXVI-33.

8 CDJC, XXV b-44.

understand that they will execute their instructions without balking.

An official report dated July 1, 1942, and signed by SS Dannecker and Adolf Eichmann, refers to the approaching raid and to the complaisance expected from the Vichy government and its police. "All of the Jews living in French territory must be evacuated[9] as quickly as possible, which means we must keep up the forced pace of the work, pressure the French government..."[10]

This remark should come as no surprise. For at least a year the Vichy authorities and Paris police headquarters had given plenty of indications of their willingness. Indeed, the 8th Nazi edict requiring the Jews of the occupied zone to wear a yellow star was implemented by the police departments without any problem. During the days that followed those same police did their utmost to pitilessly track down anybody who had failed to follow that law dictated by the occupier. Having accepted that highly visible badge making the Jews easier to recognize, why would the French police do an about face with respect to a larger action? The Gestapo departments didn't think they would, but it was part of their method to leave nothing to chance. One never knew what might get into those Frenchmen who had never been expected to be so accommodating in hunting down Jews.[11]

_____

9 "Evacuated" was part of the Nazi code language and clearly means "deported." Semantics plays an important role in this repression, and the French police don't shy away from using it in the camps. In Pithiviers and Beaune-la-Rolande the internees are called "guests."

10 In *Vichy-Auschwitz*, op. cit. p. 224.

11 For this aspect of the racial repression, see *Opération Étoile Jaune* by Maurice

On July 2, 1942, some reservations surface from Pierre Laval. The prime minister would prefer that the raids are not carried out by the French police; he finds that "awkward." Be that as it may, René Bousquet, summoned to a "discussion" by the German authorities, ends up signing an agreement with SS Chiefs Oberg and Knochen. SS Hagen, who took notes, records the main points of this meeting, where the Nazis gave Bousquet a fierce scolding, intended to soften him up and make him reluctant to question any directives from the conqueror.

> If the French government creates any obstacles to
> the arrests, the Führer will certainly not understand.
> Which is why they arrived at the following agreement:
> Since, as a result of the intervention of the Marshall
> [Pétain], French Jews are not, for the moment, going
> to be arrested. Bousquet is ready to arrest the number
> of foreign Jews that we want, in a unified action
> *throughout the whole of French territory.*[12]

The Vichy government pretended to slow down, partially, the preparations for the raids planned by the Gestapo, but SS Dannecker made sure, at every hesitation that surfaced, to reiterate that the French police were at the disposition of the occupation authorities, so the instructions were not up for discussion. Before meeting René Bousquet to plan the great

---

Rajsfus, Le Cherche Midi Éditeur, 2002; translation *Operation Yellow Star*, DoppelHouse Press, 2017.
12 CDJC, XXV b-49. My italics.

raid, SS Dannecker, on July 4, dictated an unambiguous memo, which gives an idea of the scant independence accorded to the Paris police, as well as its increasingly dubious moral standards:

> It would be interesting to learn from Bousquet himself, how he intends to prove that the regular French police, which one knows are corrupt and understand absolutely nothing about the Jewish question, are ready to tackle that problem on its own in a way that meets Europe's interests... It is necessary to make Bousquet fully understand that the French police in the occupied zone are first of all under the orders of the commander of the SS and the German police. Therefore they must even arrest Jews of French nationality if they receive orders to do so from the Germans. [...] We must vigorously insist that Bousquet inform us without delay about the number of Jews that are presently in French concentration camps. I believe, in fact, that virtually all of them could be evacuated.[13]

The roundup of 22,000 foreign Jews in the Paris region had already gone beyond the planning stage. It remained to set the date and the operational details. After his July 4 meeting with Bousquet, SS Dannecker drafts a report about the evacuation of the Jews of France. Most of the raid's details are already worked out, without it seems, any disagreements between the two men. Overcoming some objections from

13 CDJC, XXVI 39.

Vichy, the agreement is reached regarding "the evacuation" of Jewish foreigners (Dannecker calls them "stateless") both from the unoccupied as well as the occupied zone.

On July 6, SS Dannecker sends an "urgent" message to Adolf Eichmann in Berlin. The note explains that the negotiations with the French government and with police officials have smoothed out the few remaining problems. The Nazis will brook no nuances and come straight to the point: "All the Jews in the occupied zone and in the unoccupied zone are at our disposal, to be evacuated." This note reveals that the French government is willing to go a little further than the Nazis regarding the scope of racial repression. Thus:

> President Laval has proposed that, during the evacuation of Jewish families from the unoccupied zone, children under the age of sixteen should be included. As for Jewish children who remain in the occupied zone, they are of no interest to him. Therefore I am requesting an urgent decision, if, for example, starting with the 15th convoy of Jews leaving France, we can also include children under 16 years of age. Finally, I want to point out that at this time we are only dealing with stateless or foreign Jews in order to get the program launched. In the second phase we will move on to Jews naturalized after 1919 or 1927 in France.[14]

Satisfied that they had met their match in the anti-Semites of the country they had so easily conquered, the Nazis

---

14 CDJC, XLIX 35.

were surprised by some of the misgivings expressed by their partners. Why was it necessary to protect the naturalized, the veterans of the First World War, the medal holders, etc? Finally, why did Pierre Laval insist on protecting French Jews? This backward state of mind needed to be straightened out. Hunting down Jews must be seen as a coherent whole, and the men of the Gestapo will devote themselves to enabling some picky anti-Semites to understand that there is no difference between a native French Jewish university graduate and a Polish Jew who sells socks at a suburban market.

Time was running out. On July 7, 1942, Colonel Knochen, chief of the SIPO-SD, reports with satisfaction to the high German authorities in France: "Negotiations with Prime Minister Laval, Minister of State for the Police Bousquet and the Commissioner for Jewish Affairs Darquier de Pellepoix, have produced the following results:

> All stateless Jews of both sexes, aged 16 to 45, in the
> occupied and unoccupied zones, who are not living in a
> state of mixed marriage, will be arrested. In the occupied
> zone that will produce a count of 22,000. It remains to
> be seen how many Jews fit these criteria in the unoccupied
> zone. This action has the approval of Marshall Pétain,
> chief of state and of the Council of Ministers... The
> supervision of the convoys in the occupied zone will be
> ensured by the French gendarmerie.[15]

---

15 CDJC, XXV b-52.

Also on July 7, a conference was taking place under SS Dannecker's leadership, at the Gestapo offices at 31bis, Avenue Foch in Paris. Aside from Prefect Jean Leguay, the representative of René Bousquet in the occupied zone, all the top departmental chiefs from police headquarters were there. Dannecker presented the broad outlines and methods of the raid, already all in place, without omitting the slightest detail. It amounts to a memorandum addressed to the Paris police with all of the practical aspects of the raid that it is charged with carrying out under the supervision of the occupier. (One will see, after the raid, that the French police went far beyond their initial orders.) Likewise, in the Conference report, there is a point that seemed obvious to the Gestapo men: André Tulard's department will make available to the municipal police chiefs the police registration cards of the Jews to be arrested, at the latest by Thursday evening (July 9). The raid is then set for Monday, July 13, 1942, but after some consideration it quickly emerges that the date is not satisfactory.[16]

It had become clear incidentally during the conference that Jean Leguay would have liked to arrange a more autonomous role for the French police, meaning, in the command or control of the operation and not just as the rank and file forces. SS Dannecker could not entertain that position and he stated, on July 8: "It would result in the French police no longer being subordinated except in a very

---

16 CDJC, XXVI 41. July 14 was the traditional French national holiday and thus a poor choice for a major operation. [Eds.]

special way to the occupation authorities." Followed by this reaction from the chief of Section IV B of the Gestapo:

> I told Leguay that for the moment, the situation remains unchanged and that the French police (particularly in local actions or in special cases) were obliged to carry out the orders of our local departments or the commanders of the SIPO (SD), to whom they are subordinate, without seeking prior agreement from the Chief of Police regarding the legitimacy of the orders in question. There is no room for this sort of bad attitude especially with regard to the Jewish question.[17]

It could not be stated more clearly—in this instance, as well as many others, the police of France were completely under the orders of the enemy. It is not possible to uncover any mitigating circumstance!

There is no real opposition to the *Befehl* (order) of the Gestapo. Thus on July 9, Jean Leguay lets Darquier de Pellepoix, Commissioner for Jewish Affairs, know that "the police departments will conduct the necessary preparations to carry out the police operations in the Paris region agreed to by the German authorities and yourself." Cleverly, René Bousquet's representative laid the responsibility for the operation on Darquier, while assuring his own material support. Jean Leguay continues: "The operations can be summed up as follows: arrests and assembly of 22,000 Jews,

---

17 Ibid.

(in preparation for their *transfer*[18]) of both sexes, aged 15 to 60, of the following nationalities: German, Austrian, Polish, Czechoslovakian, Russians (Whites and Reds), stateless. Jews with an Aryan spouse, breastfeeding mothers and women in an advanced state of pregnancy will be exempt from these measures."[19]

This communication from Jean Leguay is confirmed by SS Dannecker in a note sent to his colleagues in Brussels adding another important point: "The second phase of the mass evacuation of the Jews of France, as we see it, consists of insisting that the French government denaturalize Jews who immigrated after the World War, thus making their evacuation possible as well."[20]

At the Council of Ministers held at Vichy on July 10, 1942, Pierre Laval no longer has any hesitations. A few days later, in Paris, he has a long meeting with General Oberg and conveys his endorsement of the Gestapo decisions already agreed to by police headquarters and the Chief of Police, René Bousquet. The minutes issued by the Council of Ministers seem innocuous: "The Jewish question was the subject of an exchange of views between the head of the government and General Oberg." Then, this remark whose true worth must be appreciated: "In a humanitarian spirit, the head of the government obtained—contrary to the first German proposals—an agreement that children, including

---

18 Another example of language code. "Transfer" clearly means deportation. Our emphasis.
19 In *Vichy-Auschwitz,* op. cit. p. 242.
20 CDJC, XXV b-54.

those under the age of 16, will be allowed to accompany their parents."[21]

The preparations move at a good pace because SS Dannecker was pressured by his superiors to proceed as quickly as possible to the realization of the great raid. On July 10, another meeting dealing with final details of the arrest and deportation of foreign Jews from the Paris region, reports on the "evacuation of stateless Jews." SS Obersturmführer Röthke is the secretary for this working session, which takes place at the offices of the CGQJ [Commissariat général aux questions juives]. Aside from Dannecker and his underlings the French representatives at the meeting are Gallien, director of the CGQJ, Leguay, Bousquet's deputy in the occupied zone, a translator, and as the report plainly notes, "some gentlemen from the French police, a representative of the SNCF [the French railroad system], and three representatives of the *Assistance Publique* [Public Welfare Agency].

The meeting gets right down to the business at hand: It is decided to start the raid on July 16, 1942 at 4 a.m. The people

---

21 In *Vichy-Auschwitz*, op. cit. p. 244. After the raid, children were soon separated from their parents, who were the first to be deported. The pseudo-humanitarian approach of Pierre Laval is refuted by this report. Most of the men arrested during the great raid will be deported before July 30, while their children, gathered later on in the camps Pithiviers and Beaune-la-Rolande in the Loiret, with their mothers, will be brutally held back, the gendarmes wielding clubs against the mothers who were resisting this infamy. On this topic, it is essential to refer to Annette Muller's book *La petite fille du Vél d'Hiv*, Denoël, 1991, where this true crime against humanity is related. Not until mid-August 1942 will these children be sent to Drancy in small groups and then in turn, deported.

arrested must be taken to the Vélodrome d'Hiver. André Tulard has done a good job[22] and SS Röthke underlines: "Director Tulard estimates that approximately 24,000 to 25,000 persons will be arrested. The age limit can range up to 55 years for women and 60 years for men."[23]

With regard to logistical matters it is time to consider the first deportation convoy for the victims of the raid. July 21 seems like a reasonable date to the participants in this last preparatory meeting.[24]

A cable from SS Dannecker to Adolf Eichmann in Berlin, dated July 10, shows that the project has taken shape and the only thing remaining is to go into action with the mercenaries of the French police who are at the ready. "The arrest of stateless Jews in Paris will be organized by the French police in the period from July 16 to 18, 1942. It can be expected that there will remain 4,000 Jewish children, and the UGIF[25] can place a maximum of 400 in its own centers. I am requesting an urgent decision (with a telex response) in

---

22 The role and effectiveness of André Tulard in the preparation of the data files used for the great raid are reported in *La police de Vichy* by Maurice Rajsfus, Le Cherche Midi Éditeur, 1995, pp. 43, 44, 72, 106, 120 and 125.

23 On the appointed day the police carrying out the arrests will pay no attention to these nuances. There will be no age limit. The elderly will be arrested and some will even be carried off on stretchers.

24 CDJC, XXV b-60.

25 The Union général des israélites de France (UGIF), a public institution created by a law dated November 29, 1941, played a most ambiguous role until the summer of 1944, particularly through the homes that took in Jewish children of a young age, many of whom were picked up in the raid and then kept in the care of the French police as well as departments of the Gestapo. Acting on the grounds that one had to choose the lesser evil, the UGIF will indirectly help Vichy and the Nazi occupiers. For more about the UGIF, see *Des Juifs dans la collaboration* by Maurice Rajsfus, EDI, 1980, and *Face à la persecution, Les organization juives á Paris de 1940 à 1944* by Jacques Adler, Calmann-Lévy, 1985 as well as the memoir by Bernard Fride, *Une mauvaise histoire juive*, Ramsay, 1991.

order to know, for example, whether, after the 10th convoy, the stateless children (who are to be evacuated) can also be evacuated..."[26]

The big maneuvers by the French police can now begin, and the director of the municipal police, Émile Hennequin, must urgently compose his notorious decrees of July 12 and 13, 1942, preparing for the raid of July 16.[27] It is important to take note of the following detail in the introduction to this document: "The occupation Authorities have decided to arrest and round up a number of Jewish foreigners." Curiously, the document does not mention the deportations that will soon follow. In the short term no detail is overlooked. It is emphasized that the director of the municipal police has taken pains to improve the demands of the SS. Thus, although the plan prepared by SS Dannecker contemplated that French children would be taken under the custody of Public Welfare before being entrusted to the squalid Union général des israélites de France, the Hennequin circular is quite clear: "Children under the age of 16 will be taken away at the same time as their parents."

One had to be productive. Perhaps the police officials sensed that they would not achieve the number of arrests demanded by their Gestapo guardians. Thus they needed to round up young children as well as the elderly, without any heed to the age or health of the victims, whether they be French or not (that being the case for most of the children).

---

26 CDJC, XX a-58.
27 CDJC, XX a-14. The complete text of this decree can be found in Appendix 1.

After all, the child of a foreigner cannot be altogether French...

On July 15, Colonel Knochen sends a memorandum by special courier to the various German police and military authorities in France. It states, in substance: "Through its spokesperson acting with full authority, Minister of State for the police Bousquet, the French government declares that it is ready to arrest, in a large-scale action, stateless Jews in Paris and to keep them at our disposal to be transported to labor camps in Germany. The French police will conduct the arrest action *autonomously and under its own responsibility*.[28] At first, the police intended to carry out this action between July 13 and 15, 1942. But in their consideration for the national holiday of July 14 the action has been postponed until the 16th and 17th of July, 1942. The action will begin promptly at 4 a.m. on July 16, 1942. According to information supplied by French police authorities, a total of 24,000 to 25,000 stateless Jews are affected by these arrest measures. The French police intend to mobilize 3,000 policemen for the arrests of July 16 and 17, 1942. The action must be concluded by the 17th of July, 1942, at 1 p.m. The arrested Jews will first be transported to the Vélodrome d'Hiver... Everything is in place for the accelerated transport of the Jews to the territory of the Reich."[29]

Also on July 15, preparations having all been completed, and the required police in place, René Bousquet gives Prefect

---

28 Our emphasis.
29 CDJC, XX b-68.

of Police, Amédée Bussières the green light to start the raid (the Nazis call it *The Action*).

> As you have been verbally informed, the German
> Authorities have decided to transfer to territories in
> the East, Jews living in the Paris region who are in the
> following categories: stateless, Germans, Austrians,
> Czechoslovaks, Polish, Russians, refugees from the Saar
> [protectorate]. They have invited the French authorities
> to assemble Jews belonging to these categories in
> camps in the occupied zone, from which they will be
> transferred. The Commissaire général for Jewish Affairs,
> having given his approval for the execution of this
> operation by departments of the French Police, [asks
> that you] please make all the necessary arrangements
> for this purpose, in accordance with the conditions that
> have been prescribed during the meetings that you were
> called to attend.[30]

---

30 In *Vichy-Auschwitz*, op. cit., p. 259.

4

THE NIGHT BEFORE THE BATTLE

THERE ARE LEAKS, of course. It is impossible to hide an operation of this scope with preparations underway for two weeks.

"They" were warned. From July 13 or 14, 1942, a few police officers informed some neighbors or friends of the imminent raid. A few families then tried, more or less successfully, to hide, but it was late for such actions. In the end, aside from a few gestures of solidarity, the behavior of this country's forces of order was not particularly convivial, although later on, some well-intentioned souls tried to validate the myth that numerous policemen gave warnings.[1] Generally speaking, one can say that this savage raid was received with great indifference. Nevertheless the cold reception gave way to pity when it became known that children had been arrested.

After the first series of arrests of May 14, 1941, almost 10,000 men had been arrested in successive waves. But no one could foresee that women, children and the elderly would also be targeted. There had been several deportation convoys

---

1 A myth that is often repeated, including by Jacques Chirac, in his speech of July 16, 1995. (See the complete text in Appendix 3).

since March 27, 1942, but the future victims believed that the first deportees had been sent to work in Germany. Besides, hadn't the first thousand deportees traveled seated in third-class cars? The Nazis, seconded by the French police, tried to reassure people. Moreover, until the eve of the great raid, there were no deportations, only evacuations.

The Jewish institutions, like the UGIF, set up by the Vichy government with the approval of the Gestapo, or those that were simply tolerated, like the Paris Consistoire, knew the approximate date of the raid as of the beginning of July. They also had no desire to spread the alert. The most damning document affirming that astonishing failure to act is a letter from the leading official of the UGIF in the occupied zone, André Baur, to Darquier de Pellepoix: "It seems to us particularly dangerous to let the Jewish population know that it can expect a new and vast deportation operation. It is not our job to sow panic, by making it aware, even partially, of your letter, which we consider to be confidential."[2] A few days earlier, the General Commissioner for Jewish Affairs had notified the leaders of the UGIF to start supplying, with the help of the Jewish population, articles that would be needed by the deportees. Since they considered that notice to be confidential, the UGIF carefully kept the secret of the approaching raid from everyone, except from some very close insiders, while publicly denying it.[3]

---

2 CDJC, XXVIII a-31.

3 See the work of Adam Rayski, *Les choix des Juifs sous Vichy,* La Decouverte, 1992, pp. 99–103. In July 1942, Adam Rayski was one of the principal leaders of Jewish immigrant communists in the underground.

Be that as it may, warned or not, many families are overwhelmed by doubt and anxiety. Rumors are constant, persistent and becoming evermore detailed. In families that remembered the pogroms in Russia or Poland thirty or forty years earlier, the experience of persecution dampens the spirits. Anyway, there does not seem to be a way out.

Since the beginning of the year 1942, a week does not go by, or even a day, without the spread of some false news. Perhaps it's best to stay worried. The raid will happen tomorrow, maybe tonight. The warnings come from "Radio rue des Rosiers," the equivalent of the grapevine for Jewish immigrants. It's fear, constantly stirred up, often anxiety, not quite yet panic:

> The ultimate precaution would be for the men to hide. The women and children have nothing to fear. The fact is that during the previous raids only the men were arrested. And furthermore, suppose that one wanted to flee, or live in a hideout with the family... how does one do it? Most families don't have any money.[4] Command of the French language is faltering, so limited that it would not enable one to get through the first of the numerous checkpoints or to allay the inevitable suspicions. Where can one go? To the countryside, of course, provided you know someone who will take you in. To get into the free zone, sure, if you have a

---

[4] After the enactment of the two successive Jewish Laws (October 3, 1940, and June 2, 1941) most of the professions are barred to the Jews, and many families are reduced to a state of dire poverty.

smuggler, the ability to pay, to know where to hole-up if the crossing succeeds... it prevents all but a few potential victims from leaving their apartments before the police knock on their doors on Thursday, July 16, 1942.[5]

A few days before the large-scale operation, Jewish immigrant communists belonging to the organization *Solidarité*, hampered by their meager resources, warn some families that have already been traumatized. The "monster raid," say the authors of a very accurate leaflet, will not spare women or children. The flyer is a manual with instructions for survival. It is no longer a matter of defending the political rights of the outcasts but their lives. "What must every Jew do? Don't wait at home. Take every step needed to hide, particularly the children, with the help of the sympathetic French population."[6]

Very often, aside from the limited distribution of this kind of flyer, the call to flee falls on deaf ears. There are few convincing arguments when one is already in the center of the storm. Given the broad sweep of the repression, those who could have been warned do not have the wherewithal to disappear for any length of time. "To hide during a raid is possible. But how hard it is to flee Paris! Taking the train is terribly risky. You have to take off your (Jewish) star and have papers that do not have the word Jew stamped on them, because the stations are watched and there are frequent

---

5 In *Les Juifs pendant l'Occupation* by André Kaspi, Le Seuil, 1991.
6 The warning was reissued in several Yiddish flyers. A complete translation appears in Appendix 2.

police checkpoints…"[7]

At the very moment that some families are reading this final notice about the storm, the requisition orders for the buses, signed by the chief of police, are already on their way to the bus depots in Paris and the suburbs. The bus drivers are not civil servants, only salaried workers. However, none of them shy away from the requisition order: fear of reprisals, maybe, or simply indifference to the sad job that has to be done.

Witness to the raid, Roger Boussinot begins his account not strictly speaking with the operation itself but with a description of those TCRP buses whose presence in the streets of Paris, at dawn that July 16, 1942, puzzled him: "Since four o'clock in the morning, while Paris sleeps, buses and vans with blue headlights are coming out of barracks, garrisons and depots, and moving about in spite of the curfew, headed towards Belleville, Saint-Paul, Popincourt, Poissonnière and Temple quartiers. Arriving at their destinations, the vehicles are lined up along the sidewalks, waiting…"[8]

The eyewitness accounts are only interesting insofar as what they confirm, and also in terms of how the archives reveal the mission orders and the signatures of the highest responsible authorities for the operation that is about to unfold. "Around midnight, everything is ready. The TCRP lines up all the requisitioned buses in its depots. Six of those are parked as reserves in the courtyard of police

---

7 In *La grande rafle du Vél d'Hiv* by Claude Levy and Paul Tillard, J'ai lu, 1968, p. 35.
8 In *Les guichets du Louvre* by Roger Boussinot, Folio, 1980, pp. 11–12.

headquarters." Already in place: "Police vans have joined the TCRP buses, lined up along the sidewalks, waiting for their loads. The driver remains seated in the cab. Occasionally he gets out to roll a cigarette…"[9] In the end, this is a job, like any other.

---

9 In *La grande rafle du Vél d'Hiv,* op. cit., p. 27.

5

THE RAID

AT DAWN ON JULY 16, 1942, there was virtually a state of siege in several Parisian quartiers and in some nearby suburbs, like Montreuil. The object was to hunt down foreign Jews and arrest as many as possible. Or at least to get close to the 22,000 men, women, and children demanded by the Gestapo. The troops were already in place. One thousand three hundred and seventy two teams of two policemen each: 2,744 police in all from the twenty Parisian arrondissements. They were ready to surround the impoverished dwellings of Jewish immigrant families. Because it was considered strenuous work, reinforcements were dispatched, often in great numbers, to the "problem" arrondissements: 255 police to the 20th arrondissement, 246 to the 11th, 156 to the 3rd, 152 to the 10th, etc.

All in all, there were 1,916 additional police. The total came to 4,600 police, a small army for the capital city alone. Nor should one overlook the police guards, on high alert, stationed in the "primary collection" centers, accounting for another 450 police assigned to accompany the "prisoners" in the buses requisitioned for the raid. The Hennequin flyer states that 50 buses of the TCRP and 10 vans with their personnel had been placed at the disposal of the police forces.

If one adds the police charged with carrying out the raid in the suburbs, then there were at least 7,000 civil servants mobilized on July 16, 1942, starting at 4 a.m.[1] Even 9,000 is a plausible count.

All these thousands of French police agreed to carry out the job assigned to them by the Gestapo through their own superiors. There are no signs in the archives of refusals to obey. No known sanctions or disciplinary action. Only one policeman, at the Nogent-sur-Marne police station, resigned the day after the raid.[2]

THE BEHAVIOR OF THE POLICE

Rounding up frightened families that had been woken up with a start in the middle of the night was not easy. Brutality was in order because, contrary to myth, the police assigned to the raid were not necessarily going to be dealing with sheep, even though the already traumatized population might seemed resigned. Fearing desperate resistance, the police used force even though it was not necessary. Loud voices and filthy language were the rule.

"Quite often, the operations are not exactly as planned: At Montreuil, Cyria Zylberberg is in a well concealed hiding place as the police destroy her entrance door with blows of an axe. In Vincennes, the police who came to Henri Leder's

---

1 According to the analysis of the of the Hennequin flyer, in Appendix 1.
2 See *La grand rafle du Vél d'Hiv* by Claude Levy and Paul Tilard, J'ai lu, 1968, p. 244. According to these authors, some gendarmes at Choisy-le-roi refused to participate in the raid.

apartment, smashed in the door..."[3]

There are many terrified accounts of the brutality that punctuated the arrests. The victims were threatened with death without any verbal restraints in the presence of their children who were taken away with their parents.

"When we got into the van—Madame Rado recalls—a chief shouted to the officers, for our benefit: 'The first one who moves, who tries to get away, shoot him!'"

An anti-riot policeman remembers: "Our orders were unambiguous. Any sign of an attempt to flee, we were to fire into the crowd. That's what the machine gunners were there for. The people should harbor no doubts about what's in store for them. That would keep them quiet. Cut off any desire to revolt."[4]

Annette Muller was nine years old when the police came to arrest her family. Despite her young age, the memory of that brutal police intrusion has not faded.

I heard a terrible banging on the door. We got up, hearts pounding. The blows shook the door and echoed through the building. It seized my heart, banged at my head. I was shaking all over. Two big men, in beige raincoats, came into the bedroom: "Hurry up, get dressed, we're taking you away." Suddenly I saw my mother throw herself on her knees, hugging the legs of the man in beige, sobbing: "Take me away, but please,

3 In *Les juifs dans la banlieu parisienne* by Jean Laloum, CNRS Éditions, 1998, p. 220.
4 In *La grande rafle du Vél d'Hiv*, op. cit., p. 60.

don't take my children." He kicked her away. I looked at my mother, I was ashamed.[5]

A distressed child always looks for some familiar object to grab on to, a lifeline. For a little girl it's often a doll. Something that even an ordinary policeman could understand. Not so for Annette Muller: "The detective tore the doll from my arms and threw it on the bed. I fell silent, frightened…"[6]

The account provided by Roger Boussinot, one of the few non-Jews to speak out about the raid, is terrifying. The scene took place in a street of the 4th arrondissement in Paris, late in the morning. This is the Paris quartier where the police presence was most visible and brutality was the rule:

There was a howl from the depths, like a beast whose throat had been slit. Two ashen faced cops were pulling a woman who braced herself, letting her feet drag so that she would have fallen if they had not held her up. The cops had the look of animals straining under a yoke. They were not at all careful, dragging the woman by her arms with their paws. She was moaning but had stopped struggling. They were pulling her in the direction of the rue des Archives, where the vehicles were parked.[7]

Determined to carry out the mission and make the

---

5 In *La grande rafle du Vél d'Hiv*, op. cit., p. 60.
6 Ibid, p. 87.
7 In *Les guichets du Louvre* by Roger Boussinot, op. cit., pp. 79–80.

numbers demanded by the Gestapo, the police were not satisfied with the lists prepared for the raid:

> At six o'clock in the morning, there was a knocking on the door. A detective told my mother to follow him and when he saw me, he asked who I was. I was not on the list because I had not been included in the census. He simply added my name to the list in spite of the protests of my mother, who was threatening to call emergency services.[8]

There are many different accounts. In some cases, more numerous than one might think, the concierges served as informants to the police, adding to the general horror:

> At six o'clock in the morning someone is banging on our door. Surprised and worried, my wife asks: "Who's there?" Then the alarming answer: "Open up, police!" My wife had barely opened the door when shouts boomed out: "Hurry, hurry, get dressed. Take blankets and food for two days!" My wife pleads, saying that I am sick and hardly in condition to get out of bed. At that point, the police, like a bunch of hooligans, reacted even more brutally, saying that if I didn't dress myself, they would do it by force. Given the menacing situation I called on all my strength to start to dress myself. Taking advantage of a momentary distraction I was

---

8 The account of Sarah Lichtsztejn, in *Vent printanier* by Blanche Finger and Willi Karel, La Découverte, 1992, pp. 119–120.

able to get my wife and little girl out of the apartment. They were looking for a hiding place between the floors. Unfortunately the concierges saw them and pointed them out to the police. With savage brutality [the officers] brought their helpless victims back into the apartment, and then shoved us around until we could not carry anything away with us.[9]

SUICIDES

For the most desperate, the often-violent police incursion into their impoverished dwellings was the last straw of a repression that they could no longer bear. A foreboding sense of absolute horror gave rise to numerous suicides.

A witness recalls: "In the 14th arrondissement a woman threw her children out of a window, one by one, and then jumped into the void."[10]

And:

It is difficult to tally the suicides that happened that day. There's the report of a doctor in Montreuil who, before dying, killed the members of his family with a lethal injection. There are other cases, equally dramatic, of this determination to put an end to it all rather than be arrested by the police: "The police were just in time to save some people they found with gas pipes in their mouths…" [Professor] Abrams counts 108 suicides and

9 The account of Paul Grastain in *Jawichowitz, annexe d'Auschwitz*, Amicale d'Auschwitz, 1985, p. 169.
10 In *La grande rafle du Vél d'Hiv*, op. cit., pp. 51–52.

24 sick people including two women who would die during the course of the raid.[11]

In the Prefecture of Police archive in Paris there are also numerous records of these suicides. They were a significant occurrence. Hour by hour, the police departments were notified of the suicides that took place, sometimes just as the police were breaking down the doors of their intended victims.

Memo from the chief of police of the 11th arrondissement to the staff headquarters of the municipal police, July 16, 1942, at 11:30: "At 9:30, Boulevard Richard-Lenoir, at the home of his sister, Mr. Jacques Vindhem, aged 32, a Polish Jew living at 32 *bis,* rue Amelot, threw himself from the first floor window just as he was about to be arrested. Admitted to Saint-Antoine [Hospital], his condition is not serious."[12]

At the end of July 16, 1942, the police superintendent of the Saint Blaise quartier (Paris' 20th arrondissement) reports an attempted suicide in his district which he also mentions in a memo to the chief of the municipal police:

Please be advised that a certain Chava Gynuber, born December 26, 1901, in Protakow (Poland), and her four children, aged 12, 8, 6 and 4 years old, were found, poisoned by gas in their home at 17 rue Lesage. Based on my initial findings, it seems that the Gynuber woman, of the Jewish race, feared that she was about to be

11 Ibid.
12 APP, series BA-1816 (B 51).

arrested, and attempted to kill herself and her children. I had the Gynuber family admitted to Tenon.[13] The hospital personnel have sent the children to a public children's home. I am pursuing the investigation.[14]

According to a report from the municipal police headquarters, dated July 17, there were only twelve suicide attempts in Paris, leading to two deaths, on July 16, 1942.

– At 8:45, a woman aged 30 to 35 years, swallowed hydrochloric acid at 35, rue des Rosiers. Admitted in grave condition to l'Hotel-Dieu.

– At 11:30, a 32-year-old man throws himself out of a window at 62 Boulevard Richard Lenoir. Admitted to Saint-Antoine.

– At 16:45 a woman and her six children tried to poison themselves with gas at 17 rue Lesage in the XXth arrondissement.

– At 16:45 a 42-year-old man throws himself out of a window. Admitted to Tenon.

– At 18:30, at Pré-Saint-Germain, a 53-year-old woman swallows muriatic acid. She dies at l'Hotel-Dieu.

– At 19:20, a 62-year-old man collapses on the street. He dies at l'Hotel-Dieu.[15]

It seems that not all the suicides had been recorded. In

---

13 Tenon Hospital was consigned to Jewish patients from the Drancy camp since August 1941.
14 Ibid.
15 Ibid.

any event they do not appear in the necessarily incomplete archives at police headquarters. In the course of the days and weeks to come these acts will multiply, particularly at the Vél d'Hiv and at the Drancy camp. Raids will continue in Paris and more suicides will occur. Thus, on September 14, 1942, an internal memo at police headquarters reveals:

> This morning, at about eight o'clock, Miss Malé Jadlowker, born May 6, 1905, at Riga, to Judel and Sarah Brettel, a Soviet citizen of the Jewish race, a doctor at the Pierre-Curie Hosptal, killed herself with an injection of chloroform after the arrival of plain clothed policemen from the 6th arrondissement charged with executing some administrative measures.[16]

WANTING TO DO A GOOD JOB

On the morning of July 16, 1942, the operations are progressing efficiently. However, there is impatience at police headquarters. The anticipated results were a bit slow to appear. Municipal police chief Hennequin addresses the matter in a bulletin addressed to the suburban police chiefs: "I am aware how difficult it is to reach the numbers that you should be turning in every hour, especially in the suburbs. I have noticed that the numbers communicated to us were often unbelievable. I urge you to make an exact count of the persons arrested and transported to Drancy or to the Vél d'Hiv to inform us exactly as to which officer is in charge of

---

16 Ibid.

those transports…"[17]

By eight o'clock in the morning of July 16, the high command at police headquarters had begun to worry:

> The operation against the Jews started at four o'clock this morning. It is being slowed down by numerous special cases. Many men left their dwellings last night. [There are] women who are taking care of a very young infant or even several. Others refuse to open the doors: A locksmith has to be called. In the 20th and the 11th, where there are several thousand Jews, the progress is slow. At 7:30 the police indicate that ten buses have arrived at the Vél d'Hiv… at nine o'clock, 4,044 arrests.

Throughout the day, hour-by-hour, like victory communiqués, the arrest numbers are collated by the municipal police high command. Each time the numbers of men, women and children rounded up is preceded by this despicable refrain: "The *gathering*[18] of Jews taking place this morning has produced the following results…"[19] The numbers are relentlessly announced:

- at 7:30,   4,044 arrests
- at 10:30, 6,587 arrests
- at 11:40, 8,673 arrests
- at 15:00, 11,363 arrests

---

17 APP, series BA -1819.
18 Our emphasis.
19 APP, series BA-1817 (51-6).

Another series of these triumphant communiqués from the headquarters of the municipal police on July 17 reports an additional 1,399 arrests as of 5 p.m. That adds up to 3,031 men, 5,802 women and 4,051 children for a total of 12,884 people rounded up. On July 18, another communiqué and a new total: 12,994 arrests—3,061 men, 5,857 women and 4,076 children. Finally on July 21, there is a final report from police headquarters titled "Arrests of Israelites carried out between July 16 and 5 p.m. on July 20":

Men.................3,118[20]
Women............5,919
Children...........4,115
$$\overline{}$$
13,152[21]

The raid is not as successful as the German authorities had hoped it would be. The Paris police feel obliged to improve their performance in order to arrive at that figure of 22,000 "stateless" Jews that must be turned over to the occupier. It is clear to every chief of police in Paris and in the suburbs that the hunt for Jews must continue. That is the subject of a telephone conversation on July 20, 1942, between the precinct captain of the 20th arrondissement and Guidot, of the headquarters staff of the Paris municipal police. The report of that exchange illustrates how inventive the French police could be in carrying out their assigned task:

20 The number of men arrested, considerably less than the number of women, is due to the approximately 10,000 men already interned after the raids of May 14, August 20–21 and December 12, 1941.
21 APP, series BA-1817 (51-7).

Mr. Brune is continuing the search for Jews, at home or on the streets. He is getting meager results. Therefore he suggests the following: The renewal of ration cards is supposed to take place on the 22nd of this month at the city halls. The wanted Jews will have to show up themselves at the centers or be represented by someone. Would it not be possible, under these conditions, to reach an agreement with the Seine headquarters, to provide the different centers with a list of wanted Jews? If so, each arrondissement chief would station an undercover unit in the hall where ration cards are distributed, to arrest Jews. In addition, given that fugitive Jews do not have the right to renew their ration cards, would it not be possible at the same time to remove their names from the lists at each of the centers? At any rate, this matter should be taken up quickly with the Seine, as should the matter of additional police personnel to be provided to the transit chiefs to carry out the said surveillance at the centers.[22]

The Paris police were not simply obeying the Gestapo's instructions but taking their own initiatives to hand over the required number of Jews.

PUBLIC OPINION

On the day after the raid a report from the General Intelligence Service noted, for the first time, negative reactions of the people of Paris.

---

22 Document cited by Serge Klarsfeld in *Vichy-Auschwitz,* op. cit., p. 272.

The measures taken against the Israelites have seriously affected public opinion. Even though the French population as a whole is generally rather anti-Semitic, that did not lessen its disapproval of measures that it considered inhumane. This disapproval stems in large part from rumors alleging that the families will be broken up and the children under six years of age will be turned over to Public Welfare. The separation of children from their parents has a strong effect on the French masses and provokes reactions leading to sharp criticisms of the government and the occupation authorities.[23]

This negative view of the raid has to be mitigated with an expedient comment showing that, in spite of everything, the Jews seemed to be detested by the public.

There are many who think that the Jews have no right to the sympathy of the French, because they are mostly parasites, but they feel, nonetheless, that the way they are being dealt with is simply barbaric. Trade union circles seem to be waiting for more details before expressing their opinion. Meanwhile there already seem to be some signs of developing disapproval. The socialists themselves are divided: some are content to just shrug their shoulders, while others, contrarily, disapprove of these methods that provoke sympathy for

_____

23 APP, series BA-1816 (B-51).

the Jews, making them into martyrs..."[24]

On July 27, there was a new report from Intelligence analyzing the trends in public opinion. It seems that the recent measures, particularly the arrests of children, were not appreciated at all and appear far more "disturbing" than the requirement to wear the yellow star.

The arrest of foreign Jews carried out on July 16 and 17 provoked many comments by the public, the great majority of which thought that French as well as foreign Jews were targeted by the raid. In general, these measures would have been well received if they had been directed only at adult foreigners, but many people have gotten worked up by the fate of the children, with rumors going around that they were separated from their parents. Although showing little sympathy for the Israelites, people generally feel that these measures should not have been inflicted on French Jews, especially not on military veterans. Furthermore, quite a few people are not hiding their concern that these measures might someday be directed against other Frenchmen.[25]

THE RAIDS WILL CONTINUE

On July 30, 1942, SS Röthke, who replaced SS Dannecker

---

24 Ibid.

25 APP, report of the police intelligence service, "La situation de Paris" (June–July 1942 file).

as chief of Department IV J of the Gestapo, sends a detailed report to the German military command in France. The subject: Action against Jewry in France.

> In the course of an action, which it carried out by itself with forces provided by itself on July 16 and 17, 1942, in Paris, the French police arrested a total of 12,684 stateless Jews. Unmarried Jewish men, and married men without children (5,000) were sent to Drancy, to the camp for Jews, while the rest, including 4,000 children, were divided up shortly after their arrest, between the camps at Pithiviers and Beaune-la-Rolande. Since then, 4,000 stateless Jews have already left Drancy for the concentration camp at Auschwitz, in convoys of 1,000 persons each. Moreover, a convoy of Jews left from Orleans to the same destination. The Jews who are still in the camps at Pithiviers and Beaune-la-Roland will be evacuated before the end of August. A total of 13 convoys with 1,000 Jews each will leave for Auschwitz during the month of August.[26]

Having tipped his hat to the executors of the July 16 raid, SS Röthke let his superiors know that in the unoccupied (known as "free") zone, the willingness of the Vichy regime will prove to be solid as a rock. Well disposed towards racial persecution, the Vichy Police, just like the Paris police, will not hesitate. The SS man spells it out in his report:

---

26 CDJC, XXV b-35.

As a matter of priority the French government has stated its readiness to put at our disposal for evacuation to Auschwitz before mid-August, the 3,000 to 4,000 stateless Jews who are still in the French internment camps in the unoccupied zone. Furthermore, the French government will, shortly, intern all stateless Jews in the unoccupied zone, and subsequently deliver them to us.[27]

This virtual war bulletin is confirmed on August 31, 1942, in a note from the high command of the national police addressed to Darquier de Pellepoix, Commissioner for Jewish Affairs. The note reveals that SS Röthke's instructions were followed to the letter:

At the orders of the government, since August 4, we have proceeded to arrest several thousand stateless Israelite foreigners, originally from Germany, Austria, Czechoslovakia, Poland, Estonia, Lithuania and Latvia, the Territory of Danzig, the Saar, and Russia (including individuals of Soviet nationality). Thus far, 11,184 Israelites have been apprehended and reassembled, of whom 6,340 have already been sent to the occupied zone, while the others are currently being transported.[28]

Furthermore, the Vichy police chief, René Bousquet, who signed this memorandum, to demonstrate Vichy's willing cooperation, made clear that racial repression had

---

27 Ibid.
28 CDJC, CV 61.

only just begun in the unoccupied zone.

In addition, instructions have been given to the regional prefects to step up police operations to round up the Israelites targeted by these measures who have so far managed to escape. These *individuals*[29] will subsequently be sent to the camp at Rivesaltes, from which they will later go on to the occupied zone.

At 3:30 p.m. on August 26, a memo from Bousquet's department reports the preliminary results of the previous days' raids in the unoccupied zone at Limoges, Lyons, Clermont-Ferrand, Nice, Montpellier, Marseille and Toulouse. These operations round up only 3,220 of the 14,000 anticipated.[30] [To this 3,220] the author of the memo adds the "residue" left in the camps, some 600 additional prisoners. These are preliminary numbers. By 8:30 p.m. that same day, the numbers of arrests in the southeastern départements alone add up to 848.[31]

As determined by Vichy, the national police departments as well as departmental and regional prefects are involved in these operations. Initially, the German authorities had demanded that only German and Austrian Jewish nationals in the camps of the non-occupied zone be handed over, as specified in Article 19 of the armistice convention of June 22,

---

29 Our emphasis.
30 The difference between this (14,000) and the figure of 11,184 cited by Bousquet is explained by the fact that it is based on the number of Jews taken from camps, like Gurs, and not persons rounded up in the cities.
31 See *Vichy-Auschwitz*, pp. 363–364.

1940. Other large-scale raids would take place in 1943 and 1944.

Archival sources reveal that the raids in Paris would continue at a steady pace. Some internal memos from police headquarters reveal that on September 14, 1942: "New operations to roundup Jews carried out today by the municipal police produced the following results by 9 a.m.: 59 men, 70 women, 13 children, for a total of 136 arrests." A score that improved during the course of the day... by September 15 there were 71 men, 109 women and 27 children, for a new total of 207 arrests. It is not possible to determine in which Paris arrondissements these mini-raids took place.[32]

On July 16 and 17, 1942, a number of nationalities were spared in the raids. That oversight is rapidly corrected. On September 22, 23 and 24, Jews from Romania are arrested in Paris, and SS Röthke reports with great precision: "On September 24, at 6 p.m., 1,594 Jews of Romanian nationality have been arrested. The execution of the arrests is not yet complete; it will continue."[33]

On November 4 and 5, 1942, it's the turn of the Greek Jews, the majority from Salonika, to be caught up in the storm: 1,060 men, women and children are arrested. Most of them live in the 11th arrondissement, near the rue de la Roquette. On November 5, SS Röthke expresses his satisfaction with that operation: "Based on observations of the previous actions, this result must be considered very

32 APP, series BA-1817 (B51-6).
33 CDJC, XXVL 175-a.

good. It seems that this time, the French police kept the news of this raid secret until the very last moment, as they had been told to do. *We should see to it that police headquarters is informed of our gratitude for this work...*"[34]

In between the big raids, sporadic operations multiply, but it is impossible to record all of them. On occasion, SS Röthke does not consider it beneath him to get personally involved in the hunt for Jews, in the company of the French police.

Some memos from police headquarters report on the collaboration between the German and French police departments:

> Lieutenant Röthke, employed at the office at 31 *bis,* Avenue Foch (Passy, 54-18), assisted by two French auxiliaries acting as detectives, during the night, arrested 76 Jews at 39, rue des Blanc-Manteau and 10-12 rue des Deux-Ponts; 29 men, 31 women and 15 children, of whom 58 were French, 12 Polish and 6 Russian were taken to the IVth Jail at Place Baudoyer, where they were turned over to the custody of the AA.[35]

One of those memos makes it clear that not only are French Jews being arrested, but that the age limits in effect for the raid of July 16, 1942, are null and void:

---

34 CDJC, XXV 51-a. Our emphasis.
35 Jail No. IV was the police station for the 4th arrondissement. AA stands for *autorités allemands* (German authorities). [Eds.]

These arrests affected people of all ages, from babies of 4 years old to the elderly of 66 years of age... Lieutenant Röthke said that one needn't worry about nationality and furthermore, a dozen similar operations were taking place in Paris at the same time. Staff has received no other information relative to these arrests of Jews.[36]

THE MALCONTENTS

During troubled times, there are many incentives to crime. In the hallways of power, and particularly in the field, there is a strong push to step up the repressive measures. Numerous policemen try to improve on Emile Hennequin's circular. There are also those "good citizens" who hide behind anonymity to follow the pack, howling louder than the wolves. It cannot be forgotten that between the summer of 1940 and the summer of 1944, millions of informers' letters were received at the *kommandantur* and police stations. Very soon Jews became the favorite target of racist circles, and the great raid only partly satisfied the most hateful anti-Semites. The more the police are fingered for any lack of enthusiasm the more likely there will be purges of the ranks.

The following letters from deranged collaborators fill out the picture of a country where resistance is not yet a significant phenomenon.

Letter dated July 16, 1942

It is reported that Jewish women were the majority of those rounded up this morning. The men, warned in

36 APP, series BA-1817 (B 51-7).

time, slipped away last night, thinking that it would be the same this time as it had been in the past. Namely, that with them having disappeared, their women and children would be left in peace. It has also been pointed out that many Jews did not respond when the police were knocking at their door, and since the latter did not have orders they did not break in. One policeman told me: "If they had given us the authority we could have found all those Jews who were hiding out in their homes."

I can report that this morning, when a policeman came looking for the Jews Wistock, Staham and Osorovitch, at 70 rue de Bondy, he did not find anybody. Mysteriously warned last night, they were all gone. They have managed to slip through the net several times. For some time now they have come back laughing, claiming that they have "friends" at the prefecture. It must be true because they have been able to run away before every raid.[37]

It seems that this letter, like the one that follows, must have been received at one of the Paris Gestapo departments, because it is annotated in the margins with barely legible comments in German.

Letter dated July 17, 1942
    The way in which the roundup of Jews was carried out is scandalous.

---

37 CDJC, XXV b-74.

1. There were very few Jews arrested because they had all been warned the day before, and until midnight, there was a steady coming and going of Jews carrying their valuables. To get by unnoticed they had removed their stars.

Most of them went to hide with their neighbors, some of them quite far from where they lived; for instance, the Jew Wistock who lives at 70, rue de Bondy (10th), was not home when the police arrived like most of his co-religionists, *but he, no less, continues to have his milk picked up at the dairy (by a French woman) at 76 rue de Bondy, where he is registered, proving that he must be hiding nearby.*[38]

2. The police were a disgrace. To be precise, they put on a production bound to spur French pity for the fate of the Jews and to arouse the French even more against the Germans. One heard nothing but hateful words directed at them from all the propagandists who keep up with the "poor Jews." The police didn't miss an opportunity to draw attention to the Jews. For example, making the women and young children stand in front of the centers, with lots of shrieking and screams; one might think it was the Wailing Wall. The police took away the Jews' bundles, and all up and down the length of the crowd *most of the policemen were telling the French who were watching, although most of them were not questioning, that they were not acting willingly, but that they were prisoners of the Germans;*

---

38 Text apparently underlined by the recipient.

these were inhuman proceedings; this was the new order; this is what's in store for us all if the Germans win the war, etc.[39]

The anti-riot police, who don't wear I.D. numbers, used the occasion to make unacceptable remarks; thus, yesterday, one of the latter, standing in front of 167 Faubourg Saint-Martin, and trying to encourage the Jews, told them: "Don't worry, you're not going far away, the war will be over and the Boches... will be beaten, we will tear them to pieces, you will come back, they will pay dearly for this," etc. All these remarks and incitements only encourage the anti-Germans against the occupation authorities. People who share our ideas, as well as many others, say that it is unacceptable to allow the police to act in such a crude manner.[40]

---

39 See previous note.
40 CDJC, XXV b-74.

6

TO THE VÉL D'HIV

IN THE EVENING OF July 17, 1942, after two days of raids, almost 7,000 men, women and children are locked up in the Vélodrome d'Hiver, under abominable conditions. As we have already noted, bachelors and couples without children were taken directly to Drancy.

It is impossible to describe the atmosphere in the Vél d'Hiv without the aid of the indispensable testimony that bears witness to the horror of the place, all under the maximum security of the French police and gendarmes. On the second day of the great raid, a delegation from the UGIF was able to get inside the velodrome, accompanied by German officers. Immediate reactions from the Vice-President of the UGIF, André Baur, provide a terrible account:

> On the main track, a sight! An enormous crowd in the grandstands where all the seats seem occupied. Looking around, one sees thousands of people, occupying the seats around them with their bundles and valises. On the flat center court children are running and seem to be playing, chased by gendarmes whose orders are to make

them go back up in the stands. From time to time some youngsters bring buckets of water and everybody rushes to fill up their containers, their pots or their preserve jars. On the track, to the right as you come out of the tunnel, there are stretchers with women, groaning, and little children spread out... It seems like there are only children and sick people. For the entire crowd, there are only about fifty stretchers and mattresses... During the night, Chief of Staff Gallien,[1] having visited accompanied by a doctor, declared that everything was perfect and that sanitary conditions required that only two doctors be present.[2]

A clandestine leaflet was distributed in Paris a few days or weeks after the raid. Possibly, the document was written by a doctor or a nurse of the Red Cross. The scene inside the Vél d'Hiv lasted almost a week and is described here in the same tones used by other witnesses.

No water to drink or to wash-up with. The toilets, about a dozen of them, were quickly stopped up, and nobody could get them working again. They overflowed and flooded the prisoners. This soon led to a rash of fainting spells, hysterical fits, eruptions of illness and suicide attempts. The prisoners were not allowed to receive anything from the outside: no food, no clothing

1 Gallien was chief of staff for the Commissioner for Jewish Affairs, Darquier de Pellepoix.
2 Portions of a text published by George Wellers, in *Le Monde juif,* Nos. 22–23, 1949.

or medicine... We attended some cases of false labor and some deliveries. One young woman went mad and shrieked without stop. A mother with four children would not stop screaming... Over a period of five days there were several cases of madness, suicide attempts and about thirty deaths, including several children.[3]

A social worker, whose name has been lost, tried to make herself useful at the Vél d'Hiv. She wrote a letter to her father about the living conditions in this little hell designed to terrorize the victims. Her description is unembellished:

It is barbarous, something that grabs you by the throat and prevents you from screaming. I will try to describe this spectacle but take what you can grasp and multiply it by a thousand, and you'll still have only a glimpse of this reality. When you come inside the stink takes your breath away. People are crammed together, one on top of the other, with their big, already filthy bundles [...]. The few toilets in the Vél d'Hiv are stopped up. Nobody can get them to work. Everybody is forced to relieve themselves all along the walls. The sick are on the ground floor. The bedpans beside them remain full because nobody knows where to empty them. As for water...[4]

---

3 CDJC, XLIX-13. Document cited by Georges Wellers in *Le Monde juif*, Nos. 22–23, July 1949.
4 In *La persecution raciale*. War crimes information department (Office français d'édition, 1947), p. 55.

A Red Cross nurse, who was at the Vél d'Hiv from July 16 to 19, and was later deported, writes a similar report to describe the woes of a crowd abandoned to its fate:

> We lack the basics and we can barely keep up the spirits of all these men, women and children arrested at their homes, in the street and even in the hospitals where they were being treated. No sanitary facilities, no washrooms nor toilets. The water is cut off. [...] The atmosphere is stifling and nauseating, [and there are] hysterical fits, screams, children crying and even adults who were at the end of their physical and moral strength. Several crazy people were spreading panic. Many contagious illnesses, especially amongst the children...[5]

Much later on, the surviving children will have their turn at describing the horrible days at the Vél d'Hiv. Their accounts are like those of the adults, nurses or doctors, who, with non-existent means, tried to provide help to a crowd in distress.

> The atmosphere is hellish. The place was never designed to hold 8,000 people, including 4,000 children. [...] All in all one small faucet and some toilets clogged up since the morning. No water, nothing to eat. [...] Some sick people, some people who are afraid, some women alone with their children. [...] Real panic breaks out when

---

5 "Les rafles des 16 et 17 juillet 1942," the account of Mlle Mattey-Jenais, in *Le Monde juif*, No. 12, 1967.

families are separated, husbands are sent off and only the wives and children remain. [...] At no time have I seen a single German, not during my arrest nor at the Vél d'Hiv, nor between the two. It was Frenchmen who were arresting French children...[6]

One girl's recollections are of the many French police, the operation managers for the raid, security guards at the entrance to the velodrome:

When we arrived at the Vél d'Hiv, there were gendarmes, and policemen everywhere, police vans all around. There were also a few curious onlookers, and I don't remember seeing a single German. [...] There was the problem with the toilets. They were little closed sheds, like the ones you see at construction sites, with steps and a barrel alongside it. They quickly filled up, and the smell was terrible.[7]

The horror of confinement was intensified by what a number of experts have called the "aroma of prisons." This stinking odor added abject humiliation to the persecution. None of the witnesses have forgotten the sea of human waste that became more pronounced as the days went by and hope vanished:

Michel and I were thirsty. We wanted to go to the toilets.

---

6 The account of Léon Fellmann, in *Vent printanier,* op. cit., pp. 11–12.
7 The account of Anna Radochitzki, in *Vent printanier,* pp. 99–101.

But it was impossible to get through the exit corridors and like the others, we had to relieve ourselves on the spot. There was piss and shit everywhere. [...] In the stands near us, a woman suddenly collapsed, she was dead. [...] I encountered a world of adults, filthy, sick and pitiful...[8]

The same details, the same feeling of a hell revisited, appear again in the memoirs of one of the surviving children:

I will never forget that crowd, their cries, their tears. I will also never forget the stench, the heat of the spotlights. [...] It was sheer madness everywhere. There were no provisions for sleeping, nor for washing up, or for whatever it might be. [...] Add to this, thirst, hunger, screams, the inability to move and to sleep, and you have a picture of the situation we were in...[9]

There is a shared impression that the detainees bathed in a sea of excrement. None of the witnesses fail to mention it. Medical care was rare to be found. One could die in that Vél d'Hiv, or commit suicide there:

The worst thing was not being able to go to the toilet. I quickly began to feel filthy. Not being able to behave properly, to privately take care of your basic needs, seeing people around you vomiting from anxiety. [...]

8 In *La petite fille du Vél d'Hiv* by Annette Muller, op. cit., pp. 89–94.
9 The account of Hélène Zytnicki, in *Vent printanier,* pp. 154–155.

> A few times I saw, a ways off from us, where there was
> a handrail, bundles of clothing, falling, whirling down.
> [...] It was only later on that I realized that those bags
> of falling clothes were women committing suicide with
> their children in their arms..."[10]

One last witness, among others, who wrote a memoir of his stay in this place, turned hideous by the unwillingness of its torturers to extend a bit of human consideration to their victims:

> I hear bawling, I hear crying, there isn't much to eat,
> nothing to sleep on, no way to wash up, and peepee-caca
> has become very difficult. It accounts for the foul smell.
> It is a very difficult time. You have to sleep sitting up,
> your head on your knees. [...] Down below I think I see a
> woman giving birth and some people carrying her on a
> stretcher. I see some people having hysterical fits, rolling
> on the ground. The Vél d'Hiv burns into my memory,
> very detailed and muddled at the same time, a bit like
> a black and white movie, because I see only some white
> faces and the amphitheater where everything is black...[11]

ESCAPES

Most of those who managed to escape from the Vél d'Hiv were children. On rue Nélaton, where the entrance to the velodrome was located, police and gendarmes kept strict

---

10 The account of Rosette Shalit, in *Vent printanier*, pp. 37–39.
11 The account of Joseph Weismann, in *Vent printanier,* pp. 72–73.

watch but there was always a weak point. Lazare Pytkowicz took advantage of one. This fourteen-year-old boy asked his parents for permission to try and escape. His mother answered with a flat out no. His father let himself be swayed.

> My idea was to pass myself off as a resident of rue
> Nélaton. The velodrome took up one side of the street.
> The other side was all middle class apartment buildings.
> [...] I started by discreetly removing my yellow star,
> then I went over to the entrance doors. Two guards,
> with their muskets, were always on duty, but they were
> wrestling with at least a hundred mothers, their babies
> in their arms, who were asking for milk, or at least
> something to drink for their children. [...] The two men,
> completely overwhelmed, were totally focused on trying
> to get the women back inside the place. I seized the
> moment to slip away into the street and dash down the
> sidewalk...[12]

In spite of his young age Lazare Pytkowicz will join the Resistance.

On rare occasions, people escaped in twos: a daughter, followed by a mother. What might have happened if all 7,000 had tried their luck, together? That's the stuff of fiction. The quartier was under a veritable state of siege. The terror stricken crowd, crushed by a stroke of fate, was quite incapable of trying whatever it might be, collectively. That's why escapes were rare, stealthy and always risky. An

---

12 The account of Lazare Pytkowicz, in *Vent printanier,* pp. 143–144.

adolescent girl tells about the escape that happened after careful consideration with her mother. It's about her decision to act, but how many failed in their attempts?

We'll never know.

At the Vél d'Hiv, my mother was astonishing. It's quite simple, she thought about nothing but getting out. After seeing some paralytics arrive one afternoon, she knew that the stories we were being serenaded with about going to labor camps were nothing but lies, and she focused all her energy on getting us out of there. She gave me a ration card and some money and arranged for me to meet some friends we had in the 18th arrondissement. She wanted me to get out first so that she'd be sure that I would not be left behind when she was saved. […] We were able to get to the entrance door. Mother literally pushed me to the side. The policeman on duty did not realize what had happened. There was a crowd of Parisians a few steps away who were watching what was going on. I managed to join them and blend into their group.[13]

In an extremely rare turn of events, the mother of this young girl also escaped a few minutes later. Both of them were arrested again on May 20, 1944, then quickly deported to Auschwitz, from which they miraculously returned.

Was it so easy to escape from the Vél d'Hiv? The exam-

---

13 The account of Sarah Montard, in *Le fichier* by Annette Kahn and Robert Laffont, 1993, pp. 126–127.

ples cited might enable one to think so, but the opportunities were rare indeed. As in all extraordinary circumstances, reality was often stranger than fiction. There were those who were never able to escape, and those who quietly got out and then came back:

> From the very first day, Bernard Goura and Albert Baum thought that they had to do something. They tried their luck with the young Pétainistes.[14] They were not mistaken. They got some uniforms ... for some money. Be that as it may, the two young Jews, properly dressed, had no problem getting out of the Vél d'Hiv. They went home and came back with provisions and medicines for their families.[15]

THE EVACUATION OF THE VÉL D'HIV

The raid was barely over, but the fate of the 13,000 arrested Parisian Jews was already sealed. That is evident in a July 18 letter from SS Lischka to the German military commandant in France:

> Six thousand men and women, single, or without children, were immediately sent on to Drancy, from where they will be deported to a labor camp in the Reich in trains of 1,000 persons each, within the next two weeks. The rest of the apprehended Jews, particularly,

---

14 Some groups of the "Marshall's Youth" were present inside the Vél d'Hiv with the nurses of the Red Cross.
15 In *La grand rafle du Vél d'Hiv*, op. cit., p. 143.

the women and children, are housed at the Vélodrome d'Hiver. That group will be transported in the coming days to Jewish camps in Pithiviers and Beaune-la-Rolande. No decision has been reached regarding the possibility of deporting the children to the Reich. The medical and food requirements of the arrested Jews are under the charge of the French authorities.[16]

Beginning on July 19, the pace accelerates. The prisoners of the Vél d'Hiv—women and children—are sent off as often as possible in groups of at least 1,000 to the camps in the Loiret. At the same time, the first deportation convoys to Auschwitz have already been organized at Drancy. The archives of the police headquarters have preserved the path of these transports from one detention center to another, always under the watch of the French police:

July 19, 1942. At 8:45 this morning, the first convoy of Jews, consisting of 26 railway cars and containing 1,073 people, including 50 men, the rest being women and children, left the Gare d'Austerlitz for Beaune-la-Rolande, escorted by a commandant of the gendarmerie and 24 gendarmes. A second convoy left from the same train station for Pithiviers at 11:05. Escorted by an officer of the gendarmerie and 24 gendarmes, this convoy contained 1,111 Jews, including 50 men, the rest being women and children. No incidents to report.[17]

16 CDJC, XXV b-80.
17 APP, series BA-1817 (B 51-6).

Similar reports will follow. The text hardly changes in the coming days except that the number of children is reported because they make up half of the people in the convoys:

July 21, 1942. At 8:45 this morning, the first convoy of Jews, consisting of 26 railway cars and containing 1,199 people, including 521 children, left the Gare d'Austerlitz for the camp at Pithiviers, escorted by 26 gendarmes under the command of a warrant officer. Some doctors and nurses of the Red Cross accompanied the convoy. Before the departure the *Sécours nationale* distributed a half-liter of milk per person. No incidents to report.

July 21, 1942. At 11:05 this morning, a second convoy of Jews, consisting of 26 cars, containing 1,143 persons, including 542 children, left the Gare d'Austerlitz for the camp at Pithiviers, escorted by 26 gendarmes under the command of a warrant officer. On the departure platform, the *Sécours nationale,* under the direction of General Secretary M. Guinot, distributed a half-liter of milk to each person.

July 22, 1942. 5th division of municipal police: The last convoy of detained Israelites left the Gare d'Austerlitz at 8:45 a.m., with 877 persons, including 428 children, for Beaune-la-Rolande. The total number of Jews transferred from the Vél d'Hiv to the Loiret during the course of the last four days comes to 7,618, of whom

4,544 were sent to Pithiviers and 3,074 to Beaune-la-Rolande. E.M. notified. Signed Zimmer. 8:45.[18]

On July 22, an internal memo coming from the office of the prefect of police provides a grim summary of the end of the transfer operation: "The Vél d'Hiv is evacuated. 50 sick Jews and lost objects remained behind. *The whole lot*[19] has been sent to Drancy."

To bring the matter of the transfer of the "guests" from the Vél d'Hiv to the Loiret camps to a close, Émile Hennequin, director of the municipal police, sends a detailed letter to the director of the sales department of the SNCF [the national railway train service] to remind him of the details of the above operations, with a cold precision that rivals the efforts of Department IVB of the Gestapo:

> The Jews traveled in covered cars. They were escorted by an officer and 24 gendarmes who took seats in 3rd class and returned to Paris after each trip with the empty cars. I cannot tell you the exact number of cars used for each of the trips, but I think that the central Scheduling department of your company has sent you that information. [...] I would be greatly obliged if you would kindly send the invoices for the various trips, of the escorts and the Jews to Pithiviers and Beaune-la-Rolande, to the Ministry of the Interior.[20]

---

18 Ibid.
19 Our emphasis.
20 Ibid.

7

THE DIRECTORS OF THE GREAT RAID

PIERRE LAVAL, head of the government since April 18, 1942

RENÉ BOUSQUET, chief of police of Vichy[1]

JEAN LEGUAY, René Bousquet's representative in the occupied zone

AMÉDÉE BUSSIÈRES, prefect of police in Paris

JEAN FRANÇOIS, chief of the *police generale,* in charge of the internment camps and director of Jewish Affairs

ÉMILE HENNEQUIN, chief of the municipal police

GUIDOT, staff Superintendent of the municipal police

ANDRÉ TULARD, sub-director of the Department of Foreigners and Business at police headquarters, in charge of the Jewish file

LOUIS DARQUIER (KNOWN AS PELLEPOIX), commissioner general for Jewish matters

PIERRE GALLEN, Darquier's chief of staff, later director of the police for Jewish matters

---

1 For more about the career of René Bousquet, principal partner of the Gestapo, who commanded the police force and the riot police from April 1942 until the end of December 1943, see Pascale Froment's, *René Bousquet,* op. cit. On the Oberg/Bousquet accords relating to the great raid of the Vél d'Hiv, see *Vichy-Auschwitz*, Vol. I, by Serge Klarsfeld, op. cit., and *La Police de Vichy* by Maurice Rajsfus, op. cit.

JACQUES SCHWEBLIN, director of the police for Jewish matters

GARNIER, sub-director of supply for the Seine prefecture

Their Nazi interlocuters

KARL OBERG, supreme chief of the SS and German police in France

HELMUT KNOCHEN (OBERG'S DEPUTY), assisted by SS Théo Dannecker for Jewish matters, later by Heinz Röthke

8

WHAT THE PRESS WAS SAYING

RACIAL REPRESSION HAS its own logic. In some circumstances reporting of these barbarous actions need not shock the broad masses of the French people. For the first time, women, children and the elderly were rounded up, sometimes under the eyes of next-door neighbors and local residents. The spectacle of buses crammed with pariahs did not escape the gaze of passersby. Nonetheless, there was silence about the event in the press. It is clear that instructions were given to the press to keep quiet about the raid. All intended to let people believe that the Jews, although having a rough time with the recent ordinances, continued to live a privileged life, and it was time to apply the law. The press had given a lot of coverage to the first mass arrests of May 1941, then to the wearing of the Jewish star in June 1942, but after the roundup of July 16 and 17 it was quite subdued.

Nonetheless it seemed advisable to prepare Parisians for the brutal expulsion of thousands of Jewish foreigners as the same fate would soon affect native French Jews. Thus we find the article on June 5, 1942, in *Gringoire,* under the byline of Philippe Henriot: "Rid us of the Jews!" and the future minister of information issued this charge in the form of a warning: "The police have confirmed that 80% of attempted murders in the Paris regions are the work of Jews, most of them foreigners."

Je suis partout stands out in the role of inciter to repression. On July 10, less than a week before the roundup, P.A. Cousteau, continuing his imprecations against men and women who already knew that they had a lot to fear since they had been decorated with that infamous badge:

> Have the Jews, as we demanded, been relegated to
> the status of prisoners of war? Have they at least been
> put on the same footing as our unfortunate comrades,
> prisoners in the stalags? Have they been driven back to
> the ghettos? Have they been banned—as the PPF [Parti
> populaire français; French Popular Party] demanded—
> from the swimming pools, the stadiums, cafés, the
> promenades where they sprawl, their star displayed with
> the air of a conqueror? No. The Jews of the occupied
> zone have a piece of yellow fabric on their breast that
> enables them to shamelessly play the martyr. And those
> in the unoccupied zone have nothing at all. Not even
> that!

On July 14, 1942, in the course of a traveling exhibit called "The Jew in France," then passing through Nancy, the director of *Notre Combat,* André Chaumet, gave a lecture titled "The Jewish question in France and throughout the world, the basic problem for the future of mankind." To say that there was a strong effort to condition the population for blatant racial repression and the operations to come is an understatement.

The Parisian newspapers of July 16, 1942, were being delivered at the time the roundup began. They all have the same tone but some news, mostly buried, is of interest, *a posteriori*. To wit, in the afternoon of July 15, Pierre Laval, head of the Vichy government, passing through Paris, speaks to Darquier de Pellepoix, Commissioner for Jewish Affairs, and the police prefect, Amédée Boussières. High on their list of concerns is the problem of supply: there is very little meat, fruits and vegetables; only potatoes are still arriving regularly. Newspapers in both zones announce that German troops are advancing rapidly on the Eastern front. Voronej is surrounded. Rostov threatened. The armies of Marshal Timoshenko are in flight and the road to the Caucasus is opened. In North Africa, fierce battles are developing at El Alamein. All the newspapers carry big headlines about the departure of French volunteer workers to Germany. The pace is stepping up: 14,000 on July 15 and 16 alone.

That July 16, 1942, one learns about the death of an eminent figure of the libertarian movement, Sébastien Faure. Most of the newspapers announce the "death of the old, militant revolutionary and pacifist." Even *Le Figaro*— published in Lyon—chimes in on this strange concert.

The Théâtre de Paris is presenting Marcel Pagnol's *Topaze*. The bill at Le Théâtre des Mathurins is, curiously, *Dieu est innocent* [God is innocent]. There is a revival of

Tartuffe at the Comédie Française. Among the new films at the movie theaters are *Signé illisible* and *La piste du Nord*.

In *Le Cri du peuple,* following a vicious article demanding that Jews be required to work in the fields, a particularly violent letter from a reader rails against that proposal:

> The Jews to the fields. I protest against that idea. The
> Jew, who loathes the land and the labor it entails, must
> be allowed no place in the field. He would be an agent
> of dangerous ferment and besides he would not do any
> work. So, no Jews in the fields, and since we're in such
> precarious shape, no bread for the Jewish parasite. The
> Jew should not pollute our soil or its bounty. Besides,
> why not drive him out of France...

As the roundup was starting in Paris and in the suburbs, *Le Matin* publishes an editorial by Georges Montandon (professor of ethnology at the school of anthropology) under the headline "The citizen and the inhabitant," containing some convivial gems:

> One sees a certain number of Jews with 100% Judaic
> features, who have nonetheless managed to qualify as
> French. It should be possible, based on a combined
> genealogical-racial examination, to downgrade them to
> the status of inhabitants, or nationals of their lineage
> who have not succeeded through appropriate unions to
> rid themselves of their native characteristics and thus
> acquire the features and ways of the French citizen.

By and large the dailies of both zones do not provide any more news the day after the roundup, but also they do without anti-Semitic attacks. That is the case with *La France socialiste*, *Paris-Soir*, and *L'Oeuvre*. However, on July 17, *Les Nouveau Temps*—of Jean Luchaire—prints an editorial titled "Towards a French racism," written when all the editorial staff already knew about the roundup:

> In the shadow cast by the Jewish question, the problem
> of Jewish and French crossbreeds remains unsolved.
> Some radically minded anti-Jews consider half-Jews as
> bad as Jews, and, particularly, demand that the former
> be obliged to wear the yellow star. The Commission
> for Jewish Affairs inherited from the earlier leadership
> a doctrine that regards baptism as the dividing line
> between bad and good half-Jews. For a racist, neither of
> the two policies is right.

In the unoccupied zone, *Le Figaro, Le Mot d'Ordre* (from Marseille), *L'Avenir du Plateau central* (Clermont-Ferrand), all ignore the roundup. Only *La Croix* (published in Lyon) provides some fairly accurate news on July 18, 1942, under the byline of Pierre Limagne: "The men were packed in on one side, waiting to be deported. The women were on the other. There were poignant scenes at the moment when members of the same family were separated."

A memo from SS Röthke, dated July 18, enables one to understand the silence of the collaborationist press about the roundup.

On several occasions since July 16, 1942, the French press has approached the Propaganda Department, expressing a desire to provide an account of the roundup. They were told, at the Department, that for the moment and until further orders, there should be no reporting about the action. Since other actions are foreseen later on, it would be best that only articles of a very general nature are published and these should be approved in advance by the Propaganda Department. These articles could endeavor to portray the arrogance which Jewry, far from mending its ways, continues to display now, as before, an arrogance that has made it necessary to take strong measures. They would point out that basically, we arrested Jews who were engaged in black market activities, forging passports and identity cards, bribery, all types of large-scale trafficking and other crimes.[1]

On July 18 *Le Matin,* along with all the other dailies, publishes the text of the 9th Nazi ordinance, restricting the circulation of Jews in public places but does not devote a single line to the roundup. The same is true of the *Petit Parisien,* which warns offenders against the new constraints imposed upon the Jews, that "police measures, particularly internment in Jewish camps, could be added to or substituted for penal measures." Just as the first deportations began from Drancy, Maurice Yvan Sicard, one of the leaders of the PPF, writes in the *Cri du peuple* on July 21: "A Jew can

1 CDJC, XLIX -67.

change religion, political opinion or nationality but he will always be a Jew... It is because we know that the Jew is the worst enemy of our fatherland, that he is the enemy of all Aryan peoples, that we no longer want him to penetrate into our national community."

On July 22, without yet mentioning the roundup, *Le Matin* runs a bold headline on the front page: "The Jews, kings of the black market in the South-West!" On July 23, the same daily goes a step further in cynicism, this time with a front page headline over the "Practical Living" column: "Buying a Jewish apartment is a good deal and risk free." The month of July passes by without the readers of *Le Matin* being informed of the July 16 roundup. The same is true of all the dailies in the occupied zone.

One week after the great roundup, the most violently anti-Semitic newspapers begin to hint that a wave of arrests had taken place. On July 23, the Vél d'Hiv is finally emptied of its occupants. The velodrome has to be cleaned to turn it over to its customary use as an indoor track for bicycle races. For this occasion, *Au Pilori* comes out with the first news of the roundup in a particularly violent anti-Semitic piece entitled "Our children, servants of the Jews!":

> We have just received some astonishing news. Prompted by the French Red Cross and with the agreement of M. Lamirand, Sub-Secretary of State for Youth, M. Hénon, (assistant to M. Roscoüet, chief of the Commission for Youth Labor) sent out formal instructions to different youth centers in the Paris region to organized teams

of young people, children of 15 years of age, to go to the Palais des Sports (formerly the Vél d'Hiv) at the Boulevard de Grenelle, where thousands of Jews are packed in. Their assignment is to clean up the immense building, get rid of the Jews' filth, drag out the garbage, take the sick out on stretchers if there is room, carry and sort provisions, etc. For two days this disgraceful work has been done by some of the youth centers. But now they are in revolt, and several leaders are refusing to allow the French youths entrusted to them to submit to this odious bondage.

The violently anti-Semitic bulletins take the place of information, as a signal to the French that a watchful eye was observing the purity of the race both in France and Germany. On July 23 *La Gerbe,* the news weekly published by Alphonse de Châteaubriant, writes:

Israel has figured out how to take advantage of the yellow star. They exploit it, just like everything else, and rather cleverly. They act persecuted, they pretend to be martyrs. Instructions are given with consummate skill. They take flight with the wind, spurred by a thousand anonymous voices that spread them amongst the people waiting in lines, in the maids' quarters, talking about the children to soften up the sensitive and gullible good Aryans. Poor little innocent Jews, they babble, think about their misfortune. They hawk accounts of dramatic scenes in which women and children play the leading roles. These good souls forget what the father of these kids—who will grow up—made of our France, before plunging it into war: a cesspool where our traditions languished and our virtues went to rot. The yellow star is perhaps the only means of stopping the star of Israel from taking over our entire sky.

This cynical view, at the very moment when young children are being brutally separated from their mothers in the camps at Pithiviers and Beaune-la-Rolande, is easily surpassed by an editorialist for *Aujourd'hui,* a daily that usually avoids vicious anti-Semitism. On July 24 a short column, "Should the restaurants operated by National Aid become a refuge for Jews?" confirms that there are no humanists in the collaborationist press.

Jews are banned from restaurants. Everybody knows that. And nobody is thinking of disobeying that measure. How did it happen, given these regulations, that National Aid restaurants provide good meals to Jews, agree to serve them, particularly in the rue de Lille? Is National Aid privileged, or a beneficiary of preferential treatment? We believe it's nothing of the sort. In spite of their lofty title, our restaurants are subject to the same regulations as Parisian restaurants. So?

The (unwritten) answer: Those who escaped the roundup must starve. The informed reader of *Aujourd'hui* knew how to decipher this prose.

Je suis partout shares the anti-Semitic frenzy with *Au Pilori*.

Like its colleagues, this weekly did not report the roundup, but afterwards its venomous tirades would proliferate. Witness a full page article on July 24 by the great expert P.A. Cousteau, headlined suggestively, "Pity the Aryans!" and targeted directly at the children:

> The Jewish kid wearing the star did not want the war, but he could be the Jean Zay[2] or the Bela Kun[3] of tomorrow. That old Jewish woman looks harmless but she might have given birth to a Nathan or a Mandel.[4] [...] All those "pitiful Jews" without regard to age, sex, nationality or social status, they quivered with excitement at the outbreak of the war that was to have abolished Hitlerism and which almost finished off France.

On July 31, in the same paper, a certain Dorsay brings up the roundup in veiled terms: "The rabble of the ghettoes of Poland and Germany know all the tricks. They arouse the pity of the Catholic world with their misfortunes. Kind souls, they cry for those 'poor Jews' who were torn from their homes."

Also in *Au Pilori,* in the same style, one encounters a

---

2 Minister of Public Education in the Popular Front government. He was assassinated by the Milice in Darnand in July of 1944.
3 Founder of the Hungarian Communist Party and leader of the revolution in that country in 1919. Later one of the organizers of the Third International.
4 A former colleague of Clemenceau, Minister of the Interior in 1940 in the Paul Reynaud cabinet, he was also assassinated by the Milice in June 1944.

justification of the hunt for Jews. No direct mention of the roundup. It's a matter of measures, like the good housekeeper who never forgets to stock up her cupboards with packets of mothballs.

Perhaps some, after the recent measures against the Jews, would consider the problem solved. But today, as in the past, the Jew is everywhere. He always poisons the domestic policy of nations as well as their foreign relations. [...] One of the difficulties in the hunt for Jews is the quality of their camouflage. We are familiar with the mimetic abilities of the Jews but the National Revolution has accelerated its development. [...] Hence we will not pursue the Jews with words but with more reliable means. Our doctrine has made us fanatical. We will not be half-hearted.

In *L'Appel* of July 30, 1942, Pierre Costantini would have his readers believe that the roundup had not yet happened. His words seethe with passionate hatred:

We can no longer silence the necessary cry of alarm. *Protect us from the Jews,* Monsieur le Maréchal. *Strike the Jews,* Monsieur le Maréchal. *Take France back from the Jews,* Monsieur le Maréchal. [...] In the name of the French fatherland, in the name of the French family, make the Jews do French labor. Give the poor French the wealth stolen by the Jews. Brand the Jews of the unoccupied zone and of the Empire with the yellow star. Chase them out of the French community, Monsieur le Marechal. That will be a great victory for France.

When the majority of the Jewish foreigners rounded up on July 16 had already left for Auschwitz—been "evacuated"—Phillipe Henriot took up his pen in *Gringoire* on August 7, 1942. He spewed his hatred under the headline "The romance of the star." The article contains some provocative statements:

Unhappy Jews? Even in the occupied zone they swagger and carry on with that pride which glorifies what others would consider a humiliation. Do they want us to start another Dreyfus affair? Not satisfied with invading our hotels, our cities and our countryside, do they want to invade our conversations? I swear, we now talk about nothing but them [...] because they have been required to wear the yellow star! That measure, so straightforward, which should delight our people, who are so proud of their race, has provoked bleating among those sensitive souls who are feeling sorry for the fate of the unfortunate, persecuted persons.

Le Petit Parisien waited until August 15, 1942, to report the roundup about which the press had remained mute for a month.

The first arrests were carried out recently in the Jewish

quarters of Paris and in the occupied zone against stateless Jews. Several thousand individuals without specific nationality were taken to concentration camps and will soon be deported.

"A big haul all over France" is announced in *Le Matin* on August 15, 1942.

Four thousand stateless Jews of the unoccupied zone were arrested and deported to a region where they may be compelled to do useful labor. [...] The same category of Jews were arrested in larger numbers in the occupied zone. [...] An authorized source denied that parents and children of Jewish families were being separated from each other.

In turn, on August 21, 1942, a reader of *Gringoire* could find some barely coherent news about a roundup taking place at some time still unknown. Here is the brief bulletin: "Towards a happy settlement of the Jewish question: we have learned that the Germans have decided to herd the Jews into Poland." On August 24 in *Je suis partout,* the previously mentioned Dorsay, with the same cautious approach in spite of the violence of his language, "officially" informs his anti-Semitic readership that a roundup had indeed taken place in Paris.

Some good souls, who are sometimes simply stupid people, are always feeling sorry about the fate of Jewish families in Paris. It is sure that certain Gaullist elements in the Paris police have exaggerated and even willfully distorted their admittedly strict orders. [...] But how can one compare the separation imposed on some Paris Jewish families with the tearing apart of French families resulting from the Jewish war? Nothing but horror all along the routes of the exodus. But none of that matters, it seems, for the French whose minds have been deadened by the London Radio, and for whom the only thing that seems to matter is the fate of the Jewish rabble camped out in our country.

This pro-Nazi journalist, although understated, does finally reveal the truth about the roundup.

In a more sober tone on August 14, 1942, *Le Cri du peuple* (Jacques Doriot's daily) explains rather vaguely that in the occupied zone measures designed to curtail their activities were taken against the Jews who have settled on the ground where our forefathers were laid to rest...

9

WHO COULD PROTEST?

ASIDE FROM THE RESISTANCE movements that were not yet influential early in the summer of 1942, there were not many institutions able to effectively protest against the roundup which was met with a wall of silence. There were few clandestine newspapers that spread the story of the abduction carried out by the French police. Only the churches, Catholic and Protestant, had some opportunities to intervene. Obviously, the formal protest addressed to the government by the Central Consistoire,[1] would have no impact. At Vichy and the headquarters of the Gestapo this plea fell on deaf ears:

> Considering that the first duty of every civilized state
> is to protect the property, liberty, honor and lives of its
> citizens, and to protect the foreigners who were usually
> welcomed to their territory, we address a new and more
> urgent formal protest to the French government against

---

1 *Consistoire central israélite de France* is an institution set up by Napoleon I by the Imperial Decree of March 17, 1808, to administer Jewish worship and congregations in France. The twelve members of the Central Consistory elect the Chief Rabbi of France. [Eds.]

persecutions whose cruelty has reached a degree of barbarism without equal in history; please try again with all the means at your disposal to save the thousands of innocent victims whose only offense is that of belonging to the Jewish religion.[2]

The official Jewish organizations, relocated to Lyon, could not expect their pleas to be answered. But the "great religions" could expect more if, perhaps, they mobilized their faithful. Did they? One thing is clear: protests were always late.

On July 29, 1942, Monsignor Valerio Valeri, apostolic nuncio to the Vichy government, transmits a message to Cardinal Maglione in Rome. The Vatican is officially informed about the roundup and of "the brutality with which this measure was carried out on the instructions of the occupation authorities. [...] People were particularly upset with the decision to separate children barely more than two years old from their parents."[3] The nuncio reported:

The event was on the agenda of the last meeting of cardinals and archbishops who discussed the advisability of lodging a public protest. The "no's" carried the day. Supposedly, they did not want to expose the tacitly tolerated Catholic Action movements to reprisals. Instead it was decided that Cardinal Suhard

2 Document cited by Serge Klarsfeld, in *Vichy-Auschwitz*, p. 295. The author of this letter, Jacques Heilbronner, was arrested with his family and deported to Auschwitz in August 1943.
3 Ibid, p. 297.

should send a letter about the matter to the *Maréchal*.[4]

Historians of French Catholicism under the Occupation do not devote a lot of time to this intervention, all the more limited in its impact because it was singularly discreet. According to Jacques Duquesne, Cardinal Suhard had written to Pierre Laval on July 16, 1942, to tell him that he "was deeply affected by the family dramas that accompanied the deportations."[5] He likewise points out that the Assembly of cardinals and archbishops, which took place in the occupied zone on July 25, had delivered a letter of protest, signed by Cardinal Suhard, to Maréchal Pétain:

> Profoundly moved by what has been reported to us
> about the massive arrests of Israelites carried out
> last week, and by the harsh treatment they received,
> particularly at the Vélodrome d'Hiver, we cannot muffle
> the cries of our conscience. It is in the name of humanity
> and Christian principles that our voice is raised to
> protest in favor of the inalienable rights of human
> beings. It is also an anguished appeal for pity for the
> terrible suffering experienced particularly by mothers
> and children. We beseech you, Monsieur le Maréchal,
> to take notice so that the demands of justice and charity
> will be respected.

---

4 Ibid.

5 In *Les catholiques français sous l'Occupation* by Jacques Duquesne, Grasset, 1966, p. 248. It should be noted that the author is getting ahead of himself because at the time the letter would have been written there had not yet been deportations among the families rounded up that same morning.

Nonetheless, this protest is quite discreet, as Jacques Duquesne states: "Every bishop is charged with informing his clergy of this unpublished statement."[6]

Only one month later, after the roundups carried out in the big cities of the unoccupied zone, the archbishop of Toulouse, Jules-Géraud Salièges, and the bishop of Montauban, Pierre-Marie Théas, intervene publicly in rather sharper terms, in pastoral letters posted on the doorways of the churches in their dioceses: "It is a matter of 'savage barbarism', of a 'flock sent off to some unknown destination with the prospect of even greater dangers'."[7]

Other clergymen, such as Monsignor Delay, Bishop of Marseilles, will make their voice heard in the open, but what is the use of protests that are in accord with the policy of the Vichy regime?

> We do not ignore the fact that the Jewish question
> poses difficult national and international problems. We
> recognize that our country has the right to take all useful
> measures to defend itself against those who, in recent
> years, have done it so much harm, and that it has a duty
> to severely punish those who abuse the hospitality that
> was so generously extended to them.

Not wishing to ignore his commitments to charity, the

6 Ibid., p. 249.
7 Ibid., p. 253. The government considered the eloquent public declarations of Salièges and Théas dangerous enough that they tried to suppress them. Some historians even believe that clerical opposition forced Laval to say to the Germans on September 2 that he would not hand over any more Jews like merchandise "in a supermarket." [Eds.]

bishop, in spite of everything, on September 6, 1942, notes that the rights of the state are limited and concurs in a way with the indignation of the two prelates from the Southwest:

> To arrest en masse, only because they are Jews and foreigners, men, women and children who have individually committed no crime, to break up families and to send them off possibly to their deaths, does that not violate the sacred laws of morality and the sacred rights of human beings and of the family?[8]

That same Sunday, September 6, Cardinal Gerlier—a staunch Pétainiste—whose role during this period is rather ambiguous, adds his nuanced voice to the choir: "The heart is anguished at the thought of the treatment suffered by thousands of human beings, even more so by what may be yet to come." Nonetheless, he quickly chimes in with the French Primates, "...we do not overlook the fact that the French authorities have a problem to solve, and we appreciate the difficulties that the government must face."[9]

There is not a unified approach in these views, solidarity on the one hand and charity on the other. The same can be said for such publications as *La Semaine religieuse,* published by the diocese of Evreux in the occupied zone, which explains to the faithful the need for racially repressive measures, citing the example of Pope Paul IV, who proclaimed measures

---

8 Ibid.
9 Ibid., p. 254.

against the Jews in the sixteenth century.[10]

On the Protestant side, the reaction is more clear, although rather late. After the roundups in the unoccupied zone, Pastor Boegner declared in a public statement:

> No Frenchman can remain unmoved by what happened
> after August 2nd in the internment camps. We are
> aware that the response will be that France only turned
> over to Germany Jews that it sent here in the autumn
> of 1940.[11] The truth is that men and women who were
> refugees in France for political and religious reasons are
> being sent back to Germany, and many of them know in
> advance the terrible fate that awaits them. [...] Packed
> into freight cars without any concern for hygiene, the
> foreigners selected to leave were treated like cattle.[12]

The clandestine press—whose means were truly limited—does not devote a lot of space to the great roundup and often is very late in dealing with the matter. Some of these little firebrands, published and distributed with great difficulty and all the related risks, do not mention the drama. The clandestine *L'Humanité,* appearing weekly, ignores the

---

10 Ibid.

11 Pastor Boegner is referring here to Germans interned in October 1939 and in May 1940 as well as those who, in the autumn of 1940, were expelled from Baden and the Palatinat. Thus at the end of October 1940 almost 11,000 persons of German origin—mostly Jewish—and designated as "undesirables," were concentrated in the camp at Gurs (in the département then known as Basses-Pyrénées). There are a number of works available about the Gurs camp, particularly *Le camp de Gurs* by Claude Laharie (self published, 1985) and *Vivres à Gurs* by Hanna Schramm and Barbara Vormeier (Maspero, 1979).

12 CDJC, CCXX 119.

event in its issues dated July 24 and 31 as well as August 7, 1942. Only in its special August–September edition does *L'Humanité* finally address the recent effects of racial persecution, although somewhat ambiguously:

> The barbaric Boches are not content with forcing the Jews to wear the yellow star. They are deporting them en masse. Oh! Of course the Jewish millionaires who are doing business with the Nazis like Bader of the Galeries Lafayette are handled with special consideration. It's the unfortunate poor who are victims of all the cruelty of the Hitlerites. On July 16 the Boches, aided by the French police and by Gendarmes, whose names we have, carried out a monstrous roundup of Jewish families. Twelve thousand of these unfortunates, now awaiting deportation to the East, were crammed into the Vélodrome d'Hiver under appalling conditions. [...] But the crimes of the Boches and their valet, Laval, do not stop there. The latter delivered several thousand Jews interned in the unoccupied zone, covering France with a dishonor that we are pledged to erase. [...] What is being done to the Jews today will be done to us tomorrow. That is why the French must be prepared to counter any attempted roundups, whether they be in the homes or in the factories. We have to resist the bandits with force. There is nothing else to do but to fight and to fight with all means necessary.[13]

---

13 In the collection of *L'Humanité clandestine*, t.1.

Combat, an organ of the *Mouvement de libération française,* appears monthly as a four page bulletin. It mentions the roundup in its August 1942 issue:

> All Jews born outside France were arrested on July 16 and 17, without any consideration of age, sex or health. Husbands were separated from wives, and children from their parents. Only babies up to two years old were left with their mothers. In the rue de la Sorbonne, a nine-year-old blind child was abandoned, alone, in a deserted apartment. Women committed suicide when they saw the police entering. The police of France did the Gestapo's dirty work. So much for the pride of the cops. Some were seen in tears, others their faces flushed with shame. [...] The scene at the Vél d'Hiv was sheer hell. Eight thousand Jews packed in, literally in their own excrement, for three days without food or drink. Some men died there. Some women gave birth. The clamor rising from that Gehenna kept the neighboring residents awake for three nights.[14]

Le Médecin français, a small paper close to the Communist Party, briefly mentions the roundup in its August 1, 1942 issue:

> The French police, on July 15 and 16, 1942, arrested on behalf of the Germans, some 30,000 Israelites, women and especially, children. [...] Children over three years

14 Collection of *l'Institut d'histoire du temps present,* (IHTP, Cachan).

old were torn from their parents.[15]

Franc-Tireur, the newspaper of the eponymous movement, informs its network of readers in a special flyer titled "Against the vile persecution." It denounces the horrors taking place in Paris. In its special issue of September 1942, *Franc-Tireur* elaborates at length on the subject and focuses its attention as well on the roundups that struck the unoccupied zone on August 26th.

> We saw here, in France, an unforgivable spectacle:
> French police forced to carry out the appalling job of
> separating children from their mothers! An entire army
> mobilized to track down and arrest poor, defenseless
> families, who were then turned over to those from whom
> they had fled. This despicable act took place right here in
> our fatherland.[16]

Some other clandestine newspapers, like *Libération Nord,* certainly published small pieces about the roundup but I was unable to review them. There always seems to be some hesitation in the accounts of the event. Thus *L'Humanité* explains that the French police *helped* the Germans, when in fact they were in charge of the entire "job," whereas *Franc-Tireur* and *Combat* report that the French police were *forced* to carry out the repression. That view was shared by *Défense de la France,* whose issue No. 20, dated July 30, 1942, bears

---

15 Ibid.
16 Ibid.

an article written on the spot by one of its collaborators, Franck Tenaille. Remarkably, the author, who furnishes many details, never mentions the fact that the roundup was carried out by the French police.

> Nazis and Nazi methods continue to make us sick. The odious yellow star clearly showed us how German rule is taking us back in great strides to the darkest days of Middle Ages barbarism. With the latest measures against the Jews, we have fallen even lower. Those who decreed them are forever condemned by all humane justice. Here are some facts:
> Rue Lacépède, a dying, six-year-old little girl is torn from her bed. Elsewhere, a woman falls in a faint when she sees the police arriving. They send for a doctor, who turns back en route when he learns that the patient is an Israelite. He says: "Let her die!" and goes home. Doctor or hangman? At the Vélodrome d'Hiver, 18,000 unfortunates sleep on the floor, without food or any aid. [...] But who cares, it's just some Jews. They're not human beings. We'd like to know who deserves to be called men, the jailers or the prisoners. Nearby, a mother is separated from her child. One hesitates to use the word bestiality because a beast does not separate a mother from her young. This is human intelligence entirely at the service of evil.[17]

---

17 In the newspaper *Défense de la France,* Presses Universitaires de France, 1961, p. 102. After Liberation, *Défense de la France* becomes *France-Soir.*

The reaction of *Cahiers* ["Studies for a French revolution"], published by the OCM [Civilian and military organization] of Maxime Blocq-Mascart, was more surprising. This rather dull quarterly was devoted to the reflections of a family of Resistance ideas but advocating "reasoned" anti-Semitism. In their first issue (June–July 1942) *Cahiers* devotes an entire chapter to "national minorities" (pp. 125–177). Given the racial persecution sweeping the country, the wording is strange indeed:

> Recently, the authorities have embarked on the road of brutal persecutions against the Jews: internment in camps where the prisoners are deprived of nourishment, barred from communicating with their families, deported, put to death as hostages. [...] The indignation animated by these measures is part of the massive resentment increasingly stirred up every day by the full gamut of German oppression. The truth is that the French firmly desire that certain situations should no longer be allowed and that should be accomplished through preventive measures rather than sanctions.[18]

(In other later articles, Maxime Blocq-Masquart will explain that, after the Liberation, it will indeed be necessary to resolve to enact a statute of the Jews of France, more liberal than the Vichy statute, but very strict nonetheless.)

Subsequently, the clandestine *L'Humanité* rarely devoted its columns to the repression against the Jews—

18 Collection of *l'Insitut d'histoire du temps present.*

undoubtedly there wasn't enough space. The communist leaders left that task to the group of immigrant activists in the Jewish sub-section of the PCF [French communist party]. An undated flyer, most likely distributed around mid-September 1942, reports on the turmoil amongst the victims of the roundup:

> The news spread throughout the city like a powder trail touching off a run for your life frenzy. All those who could, fled, barely dressed, seeking refuge with French neighbors, with the concierges, in basements and attics. Some simply refused to open their doors. There were harrowing scenes where the doors were opened or forced open. Women fainted, children screamed, and many of the persecuted attempted suicide. A mother threw her four children from a four-story window and then jumped into the void as the door was forced open. A ten-year-old little girl panicked and jumped from the fifth floor. In one dwelling that was broken into, the gendarmes found a man with the gas pipe in his mouth, already half asphyxiated. In Montreuil a doctor committed suicide by injection with his family. Similar scenes were repeated during the following days.[19]

One cannot say that the leaders of Free France were particularly worried about the fate of the Jews in the turmoil. Nevertheless in the days following the roundup, the BBC

---

19 In *La presse antiraciste sous l'Occupation,* UJRE, 1947, p. 47.

radio program "The French speak to the French" broadcast a rare live report. It was from France, containing some inaccuracies, but providing invaluable information to "Radio London's" listeners:

> Paris is living through some appalling times, with unprecedented abominations that exceed the horrors of the Inquisition. To show the world an example of Nazi barbarism, we are presenting an unbiased account by witnesses who lived through the event. You must know, dear friends, that the fate of 25,000 human beings, arrested during these days, as well as the fate of thousands of others, depends on your action. By building a vigorous protest movement through the radio, the press, and in meetings, you can help prevent the slow assassination of tens of thousands of human beings that has already begun.
>
> On July 16 and 17 in Paris, a real pogrom against the Jews took place. All Polish, Czech, German, Austrian and Russian Jews between the ages of two and fifty-five years, were arrested. The prefect's decree instructed the officers to give no consideration to any claims about the health of the intended arrestees. As for pregnant women, it stated that those in advanced stages should be spared but without any further details. The police took some children with contagious illnesses and fever of 41 degrees to internment centers.

They even took a mother with her child that had died the day before, wrapped only in a sheet.

Women were separated from their children. Thus, we met children between the ages of five and eight, left alone with their eighty-year old grandmother without any means of support. An eighty-five-year-old woman was interned because she could not prove that she was more than fifty-five years old. Two children, three and six years old, of French nationality, were taken hostage because their mother, a foreigner, had managed to escape by hiding from the police. Since the decree[20] did not state precisely that pregnant women were exempt from the measure, the officers took all pregnant women without exception. As a result, many premature deliveries took place. A woman in labor was taken with her guard and driven around for three hours in the van that was picking up other Jews and the baby was almost born during the trip. [...] The orders stated that the police and gendarmes were not to take children of French nationality. This order was followed randomly varying by quartier and individual instructions. [...]

The occupation authorities thought it best to remain completely in the shadows. French policemen, in plain clothes and in uniform, gendarmes, sometimes assisted by henchmen from some Doriotist organizations [ie. following Jacques Doriot], were in charge of this

---

20 This detail seems to indicate that the author of this report must have been in possession of Émile Hennequin's decree. Perhaps he was an officer at police headquarters or at the Seine département.

despicable job. Perhaps the arrest of little children is considered too cowardly by the Gestapo bosses. Are they afraid of the anger of the people of Paris?[21]

---

21 In *La persecution raciale*. War crimes information department, *Office français d'édition*, 1947, pp. 51–52.

10

FOR THE RECORD ...

IN THESE PAGES we have tried to limit ourselves to the hard facts. The file, of course, is only half-open. There are many more dark pages to this story. They must indeed be brought to light, sooner or later. The complete unsealing of the police archives will facilitate this indispensable task. Be that as it may, the story of these past horrors can only serve as a lesson so that younger generations will not allow new assaults on the most fundamental human rights. That goes far beyond the simple duty of remembering given the constant attempts to smooth over history, to make it seem acceptable, correct. How can one fail to react when, in a piece appearing in the fall of 2000, "The Prefecture of police at the service of Parisians," it is casually stated, "The Paris police was asked to carry out the great roundup which brought thousands of Jews to the Vélodrome d'Hiver on July 16 and 17, 1942."

At this point historical recall opens its doors to oblivion. In his book, *La Police,* Casamayor furnishes the best possible explanation for the behavior of the police, forgetting the willingness and spirit of initiative shown in the execution of orders: "In general the policeman is happy enough with just his brand name, like the label on a bottle, but he does not know what's in it. Besides, nobody demands that he should."

Appendix 1

ORGANIZATION OF THE GREAT ROUNDUP
The decrees issued by Émile Hennequin
(Chief of the municipal police) on July 12 and 13, 1942

Police Headquarters   *Paris, July 12, 1942*
Office of Municipal Police
Staff – 1st Bureau B

Instructions for squads making arrests

1) Policemen and detectives, after having verified the identities of the Jews they are assigned to arrest, should not discuss any remarks that might be made by them.

In any case, should there be any doubts, they will bring them to the Station, whose address will be provided to them by the Superintendent of Public Order, making sure that they have indeed gathered up the objects identified below. Only the Superintendent is qualified to make those determinations. In doubtful cases, the policemen will stamp the record card "to be reviewed."

2) Likewise they should not engage in any discussion regarding medical conditions. Every arrested Jew must be brought to the designated local gathering point.

3) When all the residents of an apartment are ready to be taken away, the arresting officers should make sure that the gas,

electricity and water meters are completely closed. Animals should be given to the concierge.

4) When all the occupants of an apartment are taken away, the keys should be left with the concierge (if there is none, then with the closest neighbor) making clear that the latter is to be held responsible for the safekeeping of the furniture, objects and effects left in the dwelling. In both cases, as indicated below, the name and address of the person entrusted with the keys should be recorded.

5) Arrested Jews should bring with them:
    a) their foreigners' identity card [residence permit] and all other family identity documents considered useful;
    b) their ration cards, ticket books and clothing ration cards;
    c) the following effects and utensils

2 blankets	1 set of sheets
1 pair of shoes	1 plate
2 pairs of socks	1 cup
2 shirts	1 water bottle (if possible)
2 pairs of shorts	1 place setting
1 set working clothes	1 toilet kit (razor allowed)
1 sweater or pullover	

    d) at least two days' supply of food. They can bring more if they wish, (not more than a mid-size valise containing only provisions).
    e) Blankets should be carried in shoulder straps, the effects and objects listed here above should be placed in a single bag or valise; there should be a total of two valises or packages, of which one is for provisions.

6) Children living with the arrested persons should be taken along at the same time if there is no family member left in the apartment. They should not be left with neighbors.

7) The policemen and detectives are responsible for the execution. The operation should be completed as quickly as possible, without useless exchanges and without any comment.

8) The policemen and detectives carrying out the arrests will fill out the information requested on the back of every record card indicating the arrondissement or the district where the arrest took place; "Arrested by," indicating the name and department of each officer and detective making the arrest; the name and address of the person with whom the keys were left; only in the case of the non-arrest of an individual referred to on the record card, the reasons why the arrest was not made and all succinct, useful information.

Chief of Municipal Police,
HENNEQUIN
Police Headquarters

SECRET DECREE N⁰ 173-42
to Divisional Superintendents, Superintendents of Public Order
and Suburban Districts
(CC: Department P.J.—R.Gx-Paris Gendarmerie and Guard)

The occupation authorities have decided to arrest and round up
a number of Jewish foreigners.

POLICIES

To whom does this measure apply?

a) Categories:

The measure applies only to Jews of the following nationalities
    Germans
    Austrians
    Poles
    Czechoslovaks
    Russian (refugees or Soviets, meaning "whites" or "reds")
    Stateless, meaning undetermined nationality

b) Age and sex

It applies to all Jews of the above nationalities, whatever their
sex may be, provided they are between the age of 16 and 60
(women from 16 to 55).

Children less than sixteen years old will be taken along with
their parents.

Exemptions

Those not covered by the measure are:

> pregnant women close to full term;
>
> women breastfeeding their babies;
>
> women with a child less than two years old, born after July 1, 1940;
>
> wives of prisoners of war;
>
> widows or widowers who were married to a non-Jew;
>
> Jews or Jewesses married to non-Jews, submitting proof of the legitimacy of their bonds on the one hand and the bona-fides of their spouse's non-Jewish status;
>
> Jews of Jewesses possessing an identification card of the Union général des israelites de France, of manila or light yellow color;
>
> Jews or Jewesses whose legal spouse is of a nationality not included in paragraph *a)*;
>
> parents of at least one non-Jewish child

In cases where a member of the family qualifies for an exemption, children will not be taken, provided they are not Jews and not over 16 years old.

Implementation

A record card will be created for every Israelite (man and woman) arrested. These cards are classified by arrondissement and by alphabetical order.

You will set up arrest teams. Each team will consist of a uniformed policeman and a plain clothed officer or a detective from the Security Branch or the Criminal Investigation Department.

Each team will receive several record cards. For that purpose, the record cards for an arrondissement or for a district will be delivered by my Department today at 21:00 hours.

The arrest teams should work as quickly as possible, without useless exchanges or commentary.

Furthermore, at the time of the arrest, there is to be no

discussion as to whether it is well- or ill-founded. You will be responsible for the arrests and you will examine the contentious issues pointed out to you.

You will set up, in each one of your arrondissements or districts, one or more "Primary collection stations" which you will keep under guard. Doubtful cases will be looked into by you at the Station or Stations. If you cannot resolve the matter, the parties involved will, for the moment, share the fate of the others.

Buses, whose number will be indicated below, will be placed at your disposal.

When you have a group large enough to fill up a bus, you will send:

> a) to the camp at Drancy, men or families without children under the age of 16;
>
> b) to the Vélodrome d'Hiver, all the others.

The total population at the Drancy camp is limited to 6,000. Therefore, every time you dispatch a departure to Drancy, you will report the number of persons sent to the camp to the staff, which will in turn advise you when it has reached the limit. After that the remaining buses will be sent to the Vélodrome d'Hiver.

You will appoint a proper escort for each bus. The windows of the vehicle should remain closed and the platform should be reserved for baggage. You will remind the special arrest teams, by reading to them, of the instructions contained in their orders, which you will hand over to each of them before beginning the operations.

You will also inform them as clearly as possible about the information that they must provide on the back of the record cards for each person arrested.

On the morning of the 18th you will hand over:

> 1) the files of persons arrested
>
> 2) the files of missing persons
>
> 3) the files of persons who changed their address and whose new address is known but is not in

your arrondissement.

You will keep the files of persons temporarily absent at the time of the first attempted arrest. They will be subject to further action later on.

To keep my Department informed of the progress of the operation, you must provide your Bureau with a continually updated accounting of the information requested above.

You will be frequently called upon to furnish that information.

The number of arrested persons sent to Drancy must be tabulated separately from the number sent to the Vélodrome d'Hiver.

To facilitate control, you should have one of your secretaries mark the back of each file "Drancy" or "Vélodrome d'Hiver," as needed.

FORCES AND MATERIALS

General preparations

All leaves will be suspended starting at 18:00 hours on the 15th until 23:00 hours on the 17th and all courses canceled until the resumption of leaves.

Guard duty at German establishments will not be provided, except for parking lots and underground garages, from 21:30 hours on the 15th until 21:30 on the 17th, except for rare cases of which you will be the sole judge.

Thus, the reinforcements you usually receive for special duty will not be sent.

Thus, each arrondissement can readily form the "special teams," ten policemen for the rotation brigade, and Brigade D, without affecting the arrondissement's normal services. These will be covered by the rest of the rotation brigade (whose strength, given the cancellation of leaves, will be the same as it usually is).

Policemen assigned to the special teams will be exempted from their normal arrondissement duties starting at 18:00 hours on the 15th; they will resume their usual tasks at 23:00 hours on the 17th. Those who resume their watch duties at German establishments starting at 21:30 hours must be relieved of all other duties after noon of that same day.

Special arrest teams
1. July 16 and 17 reinforcements

Departments dispatching forces indicated below should plan for normal training, as the figures refer only to the number of policemen. Police sergeants will not participate in the arrests but will be used for control and supervision as per your instructions.

2. Work schedule for special teams

The detectives and policemen in the special arrest teams will report for duty at the main Station of the designated arrondissement starting at 4 a.m. on the 16th. Duty hours are:

1) On the 16th from 4:00 hours until 9:30 hours and from 12:00 hours until 15:30 hours.

2) On the 17th from 4:00 hours until 13:00 hours.

REINFORCEMENTS RECEIVED
per police team listed by arrondissement

1st arrondissement — 8 teams

2nd arrondissement — 33 teams
11 plainclothes men from the 1st Arrondissement; 10 plainclothes men from the École Pratique

3rd arrondissement — 156 teams
Received 54 uniformed men from the 1st Arrondissement; 45 uniformed men from the École Pratique

4th arrondissement — 139 teams
Received 50 uniformed men from the 1st Arrondissement; 25 uniformed men from the École Pratique

5th arrondissement — 24 teams
Received 16 plainclothes men from the École Pratique

6th arrondissement — 8 teams

7th arrondissement — 4 teams

8th arrondissement — 7 teams

9th arrondissement — 52 teams
Received 36 plainclothes men from the École Pratique

10th arrondissement — 152 teams
Received 30 uniformed men from the 2nd Arrondissement; 55 uniformed men from the 6th Arrondissement; 12 uniformed men from the 9th Arrondissement; 140 plainclothes men from the École Pratique

11th arrondissement — 246 teams
Received 53 uniformed men from the 7th Arrondissement; 30 uniformed men from the 8th Arrondissement; 100 uniformed

men from the École Pratique; 7 plainclothes men from the 8th Arrondissement; 10 plainclothes men from the 7th Arrondissement; 220 Detectives from the Security branch

12th arrondissement — 34 teams
Received 24 plainclothes men from the École Pratique

13th arrondissement — 32 teams
Received 21 plainclothes men from the École Pratique

14th arrondissement — 17 teams
Received 5 plainclothes men from the École Pratique

15th arrondissement — 23 teams
Received 13 plainclothes men from the École Pratique

16th arrondissement — 25 teams
Received 10 plainclothes men from the École Pratique

17th arrondissement — 25 teams
Received 9 plainclothes men from the École Pratique

18th arrondissement — 121 teams
33 uniformed men from the 13th Arrondissement; Received 36 uniformed men from the 15th Arrondissement; 106 plainclothes men from the École Pratique

19th arrondissement — 111 teams
Received 38 uniformed men from the 17th Arrondissement;10 uniformed men from the 16th Arrondissement; 98 plainclothes men from the École Pratique

20th arrondissement — 255 teams
Received 10 uniformed men from the 16th Arrondissement; 200 uniformed men from the École Pratique; 250 detectives from the Criminal Investigation Division

Guarding the primary gathering Centers and escorting the buses

Reinforcements for July 16 and 17:
To ensure the guarding of the primary gathering Centers, the escort of the detainees in the buses, the busiest arrondissements will receive on July 16 and 17, the following additional reinforcements:

2nd...............................15 foot patrolmen
3rd................30 guards from the C.H.R.
4th.............15 guards from Public Order
..................5 guards from École Pratique
.....................................25 foot patrolmen
5th...............................10 foot patrolmen
9th...............................15 foot patrolmen
10th.........10 guards from École Pratique
.....................................30 foot patrolmen
11th............10 guards from Public Order
................10 guards from École Pratique
.....................................40 foot patrolmen
12th.............................10 foot patrolmen
..................5 guards from École Pratique
13th.............................10 foot patrolmen
..................5 guards from École Pratique
14th.............................10 foot patrolmen
..................5 guards from École Pratique
15th.............................10 foot patrolmen
16th.............................10 foot patrolmen
..................5 guards from École Pratique
17th.............................10 foot patrolmen
18th...........25 guards from Public Order
.....................................15 foot patrolmen
19th...........20 guards from Public Order
.....................................15 foot patrolmen
20th..........30 guards from Public Order
.....................................30 foot patrolmen

Schedule
Reinforcements assigned to guard the primary gathering Centers and escort detainees in the buses, will report for duty at the main Station of the designated arrondissement at 5:00 hours on the morning of the 16th.

Teams will report for duty on July 16 and 17:
Team n° 1: from 5:00 hours until 12:00 hours.
Team n° 2: from 12:00 hours until the end of the shift.
As for the men of the Paris Guard, they will be relieved at the discretion of their command.

Suburban districts
All suburban districts except for Lilas, Montreuil, Saint-Ouen and Vincennes, will form their own special arrest teams, provide guards for their main gathering Stations and for escort service, consisting of their own men.

As for equipment, it will be sent to you after the numbers have been communicated to *appels généraux* so that the transport routes can be organized.

In accord with the times and dates set by Paris, Chapter B, paragraph 2, the following reinforcements will be sent to you:

SAINT-OUEN: 20 uniformed policemen and 12 plainclothes men provided by the 2nd Division of suburban forces

LES LILAS: 20 gendarmes and 14 plainclothes men from the École Pratique

MONTREUIL: 25 gendarmes and 18 plainclothes men the École Pratique

VINCENNES: 15 gendarmes and 18 plainclothes men the École Pratique

Operations in the Lilas, Montreuil and Vincennes districts at 4 hours in the morning, with their own men and the gendarmes. They will be joined by the plainclothes policemen from the École Pratique arriving on the first metro, at around 6:15 hours.

Equipment:

The above ground network of the *Compagnie du Metropolitain* will send to each Arrondissement Headquarters the following equipment (which will remain there until the end of the shift):

1st.................1 bus
2nd...............1 bus
3rd............3 buses
4th............3 buses
5th.................1 bus
6th.................1 bus
7th.................1 bus
8th.................1 bus
9th............2 buses
10th..........2 buses
11th...........7 buses
12th..........2 buses
13th...............1 bus
14th...............1 bus
15th...............1 bus
16th...............1 bus
17th...............1 bus
18th..........3 buses
19th..........3 buses
20th..........7 buses

Préfecture de Police (Caserne de la Cité): 6 buses.

When you no longer have any need for the buses, you will immediately advise Headquarters Staff P.M. but will not return them until approved by him.

The department of Mechanical service will make available to the headquarters staff under my leadership, at the garage, starting on July 16th at 8 hours:

10 large police vans.

The arrondissements will keep until further advised, the small cars put at their disposal for special duty on July 14th, contrary to the instruction in my decree No 170-42 of July 13th.

Furthermore, from 6:00 hours until 18:00 hours on the 16th and 17th of July, a motorcyclist will be at the disposal of each of the following arrondissements: 9th - 10th - 11th - 18th - 19th and 20th.

Guards at the Vélodrome d'Hiver:
The guards at the Vélodrome d'Hiver, both inside and outside, will be provided by the Gendarmerie of the Paris region, and under its responsibility.

TABLE WITH THE ARREST ORDERS

1st...........................134
2nd.........................579
3rd......................2,675
4th.......................2,401
5th 414
6th...........................143
7th.............................68
8th...........................128
9th..........................902
10th....................2,594
11th.....................4,235
12th.........................588
13th.........................563
14th.........................295
15th.........................397
16th.........................424
17th.........................424
18th....................2,075
19th....................1,917
20th....................4,378

HENNEQUIN
Chief of Municipal Police

---

1 CDJC, XX 14-a.

Appendix 2

FLYERS ADDRESSED TO JEWISH IMMIGRANTS
A flyer distributed in Paris a few days before the roundup, translated from Yiddish

Brothers, sisters,

The Hitlerites are preparing a new offensive against the Jews. According to some news we have received from reliable sources, the Germans are preparing a gigantic roundup and deportation of Jews. Through increased terror against the Jews, the Hitlerites want to set the stage for the enslavement of all of France. The extermination of the Jews must be a warning to the French who refuse to accept the yoke of the occupant and want to live as free men and citizens.

Brothers, the danger is great. It is our duty to warn you. The Hitlerite bandits will not shrink from any crime. Closing your eyes to tragic reality is equivalent to suicide. Open your eyes, recognize the danger, take the path to safety, the Resistance, to life. The question for every Jew is: What should one do in order not to fall into the hands of the SS assassins? What should one do to hasten their fall and Liberation? Here is what every man, every woman, every teenager, must do:

1) Don't wait for the bandits at your home. Take all possible steps to hide and above all, to hide the children with the help of the French population;

2) After safeguarding your freedom you need to join a patriotic organization to fight the blood-soaked enemy and avenge their crimes;

3) If you fall into the clutches of the bandits, you should resist by any means necessary: barricade the doors, call for help, fight the police. There is nothing to lose. You have your life to win. No matter what, try to escape. No Jew should be prey to the bloodthirsty Hitlerite beast. Every free and living Jew is a victory over the enemy....[1]

---

1 Flyer cited by Jacques Ravine in *La Résistance organisée des Juifs,* Julliard, 1973, p. 98. This flyer, which is also cited by Annette Wievorka in *Ils étaient Juifs, résistants, communists* (Denoël, 1986, p. 149) presents a problem for this author, as she believes that the document, dated June 1942, was only distributed on the eve of the roundup.

A flyer distributed in Paris in August 1942,
translated from Yiddish

Brothers, sisters,

The hunt for Jews began on July 16th. Between
Thursday the 16th and Sunday 19th, some 20,000 men,
women and children have been torn from their homes
by brutal force. The French police, assisted by the
Gendarmerie, placed at the disposal of the occupying
power by orders of Laval, did not distinguish between
young and old, sick and well. The ill were pulled from
their beds and mothers were forced to carry their infant
children sick with scarlet fever, diphtheria, measles, etc.
They were quickly forced out, allowed only a small valise
with only one blanket. The horrible, savage, barbaric,
inhuman, sadistic scenes of these past few days will
remain engraved in the memory of Paris Jews and the
whole population. What happened in the homes and at
the collection points does not compare to the organized,
systematic mass assassination of Jews at the Vélodrome
d'Hiver where 12,000 people were packed in. It became
clear that the bloodthirsty Hitlerite bandits do not want
simply to isolate the Jews of Paris but contemplate their

total, physical annihilation. Beasts going to slaughter are treated better than Jewish mothers with their children at the Vél d'Hiv. At the beginning of the sixth day fathers were brutally separated from their wives and children, to be sent to the forced labor camps of the Hitlerite tyranny. Women and children were sent to the concentration camps at Pithiviers and Beaune-la-Rolande.

At those camps children were separated from their mothers. Children over the age of two will be put into concentration camps, while their mothers will be sent off to work somewhere in Nazi Germany.

The hunt to capture Jews is not yet over. The Hitlerian beast has begun the physical annihilation of all the Jews of Paris. Until now they were interested only in Jewish immigrants, mainly from Poland. But the same bestial plan is to be applied to other French or immigrant Jews. The beast is not yet sated. It always wants more blood and plunder. The thousands of Jews who listened to the communists' warnings were able to save themselves. Wherever the police encountered barricaded doors, wherever Jews were able to alert their French neighbors, wherever there was resistance, Jews were saved. During those terrible days the French people expressed and strengthened its solidarity and friendship. Supported by the active help of the French masses, Parisian Jews are determined to put up an active resistance against the latest deportation attempts.

Avenging these crimes is the sacred duty of every Jew. How can we quiet our rage after such a massacre of our brothers, sisters and children? Can we allow to go unpunished the crimes committed against the thousands of our families condemned to extermination? The children torn from the arms of their mothers? Their mothers will never forgive us unless we respond with hatred and vengeance. [...] One thought alone must guide us: How to do the most harm to our assassins and how to settle accounts? Today that is the wish and the will of every honest Jew, but not of that gang of dirty rats of the UGIF, who want to profit from the misfortune to roundup some souls and laborers for the brown torturers.[2]

2 In *La parole du soulèvement et de la victoire,* Le Renouveau, 1949.

Appendix 3

COMMEMORATIONS OF THE VÉL D'HIV RAID

Speech by Jacques Chirac on July 16, 1995

ON JULY 16TH, 1995, on the occasion of the fifty-third anniversary of the Vél d'Hiv Raid, the newly elected President of the Republic, Jacques Chirac, took a completely new stand from his predecessors with respect to the role of the French police in the conduct of the operation. *Le Monde* judiciously recalls the earlier words of François Mitterand, delivered in July 1992: "I will not make excuses in the name of France. The Republic has nothing to do with that... The French State, of Vichy, was not the Republic... Don't ask the Republic for explanations, she did what she had to..." We may note a point of disagreement with Chirac's speech: "The criminal madness of the occupant" was not "assisted" by the French. It was the French police, alone, who carried out this dirty job.

Chirac:

In the life of a nation, there are moments that offend memory and the idea that one's country represents.

It is difficult to evoke those moments, because one does not always know how to find the right words to recall horror, to speak of the grief of those who experienced the tragedy. Those who are forever branded in their spirit and in their flesh by the memories of those days of tears and shame.

It is also difficult to evoke because those black hours forever tarnish our history, offend our past and our traditions. Yes, the criminal madness of the occupant was assisted by the French, by the French State.

Fifty-five years ago on July 16, 1942, 4,500 French police and gendarmes, under the command of their chiefs, agreed to the demands of the Nazis.

That day, in the capital and the Paris region, more than 13,000 Jewish men, women and children were arrested at their homes in the early dawn, and assembled at police stations.

There were atrocious scenes: families torn apart, mothers separated from their children, the elderly—some of them veterans from the Great War who had shed their blood for France—thrown without consideration into Paris buses and police headquarters' vans.

There were also some police who closed their eyes, thus permitting some escapes.

For all those persons arrested, it was the beginning of a long and painful journey to hell. How many of them would ever see their homes again? And how many, at that moment, felt betrayed? Can one describe their distress?

On that day, France, the country of Enlightenment, the birthplace of the Rights of Man, a land of welcome for the exiled, did what can never be undone. Going back on its word, it gave up its wards to their hangmen.

Taken to the Vélodrome d'Hiver, the victims had to wait for several days, under the most terrible conditions one can

imagine, then to be sent on to one of the transit camps—
Pithiviers or Beaune-la-Rolande—opened by the Vichy
authorities.

But the horror was only just beginning.

More raids and more arrests would follow. From Paris and
the provinces, 74 trains would leave for Auschwitz. Seventy-six
thousand deported Jews of France would never come back.

We owe them an irrevocable debt.

According to the *Torah*, every Jew has a duty to
remember. A phrase that is often repeated says: "Never
forget that you were a stranger and a slave in the land of the
Pharaoh."

Fifty years later, faithful to its laws, but without a spirit
of hatred or vengeance, the Jewish community, and alongside
it, all of France, remembers. So that the six million martyrs of
the Shoah might live. So that the blood of the Holocaust will
become, in the words of Samuel Pisar, the "Blood of hope."

When the spirit of hatred is in the air, kept alive here by
fundamentalisms, nourished there by fear and exclusion. When
right here, at our doorstep, certain groups, certain publications,
teachings, certain political parties, are the bearers, more or less
openly, of racist and anti-Semitic ideology, then that spirit of
vigilance that drives you and drives us, must be more visible
and stronger than ever.

In that regard, there is nothing insignificant, trivial or
isolated. The racist crimes, the defense of revisionist arguments, all sorts of provocations—insulting remarks, witty jibes
—all come from the same source.

To hand down the memory of the Jewish people, the

suffering, the camps. To witness, again and again. To recognize the mistakes of the past, and the mistakes committed by the State. Do not hide the shady hours of our history, simply defend an idea of Man, of his freedom and his dignity. Relentlessly carry on the struggle against the forces of darkness.

That never-ending fight is mine as much as it is yours.

I am happy to note that the youngest amongst us are very aware of everything related to the Shoah. They want to know. And along with them, the French are increasingly determined to confront their past. We all know that France is not an anti-Semitic country.

At this moment of contemplation and memory, I want to choose hope. I want to remember that the summer of 1942, which revealed the true face of the "collaboration," whose racist character, after the anti-Jewish laws of 1940, was no longer in doubt, was, for many of our compatriots, the starting point for a vast resistance movement.

I want to remember all the hunted Jewish families hidden from the pitiless searches of the occupant and the Milice by the heroic and fraternal action of numerous French families.

I like to think that one month earlier, at Bir Hakeim, the French, freed by General Kœnig, had heroically held on for two weeks against German and Italian divisions.

Sure, there are mistakes made, there are flaws, there is a collective fault. But there is also in France a certain idea of France, straight, generous, faithful to its traditions and to its genius.

That France was never at Vichy. At that moment, she is no longer in Paris and had not been there for a long time.

She is in the Libyan desert and wherever the free French are fighting. She is in London, personified by General de Gaulle. She is present, indivisible in the hearts of those French, those "righteous among the nations," who in the darkest depths of the storm and at the peril of their lives, as Serge Klarsfeld has written, in saving three quarters of the Jewish community residing in France, gave the best that life has to offer. Humanist values, the values of liberty, justice and tolerance that make up the French identity and bind us to the future.

Speech by François Hollande
on July 22, 2012

DELIVERED IN PARIS at the former site of the Vélodrome d'Hiver, which was destroyed after a fire in 1959, François Hollande's memorial speech, commemorating the 70th anniversary of the July 16–17, 1942 roundup, shifted public discourse. This translation is reproduced with permission from *New York Review of Books*.

Prime Minister, President of the National Assembly, ambassadors, Mayor of Paris, President of the Representative Council of Jewish Institutions of France, Chief Rabbi, representatives of the religions, ladies and gentlemen:

We've gathered this morning to remember the horror of a crime, express the sorrow of those who experienced the tragedy, and speak of the dark hours of collaboration, our history, and therefore France's responsibility.

We're also here to pass on the memory of the Holocaust—of which the roundups were the first stage—in order to fight the battle against oblivion and testify to new generations what barbarity is capable of doing and what resources humanity may possess to defeat it.

Seventy years ago, on July 16, 1942, early in the morning,

13,152 men, women, and children were arrested in their homes. Childless couples and single people were interned in Drancy, where the museum created by the Mémorial de la Shoah will stand in the autumn.

The others were taken to the Vélodrome d'Hiver. Thrown together for five days in inhuman conditions, they were taken from there to the camps of Pithiviers and Beaune-la-Rolande.

A clear directive had been given by the Vichy administration. "The children must not leave in the same convoys as the parents." So, after heartrending separations, they departed— the parents on one side, the children on the other—for Auschwitz-Birkenau, where the deportees of Drancy had preceded them by a few days.

There, they were murdered. Solely for being Jews. This crime took place here, in our capital, in our streets, the courtyards of our buildings, our stairways, our school playgrounds.

It was to prepare the way for other roundups, in Marseille and throughout France—in other words, on both sides of the demarcation line. There were also other deportations, notably of gypsies.

The infamy of the Vél d'Hiv was part of an under-taking that had no precedent and has no comparison: the Holocaust, the attempt to annihilate all the Jews on the European continent.

Seventy-six thousand French Jews were deported to the death camps. Only 2,500 returned.

Those women, men, and children could not have known the fate that awaited them. They could not even have imagined it. They trusted in France.

They believed that the country of the great Revolution and the City of Light would be a safe haven for them. They loved the Republic with a passion born of gratitude. Indeed, it was in Paris in 1791, under the National Constituent Assembly, that Jews had become fully-fledged citizens for the first time in Europe. Later, others had found in France a land of welcome, a chance at life, a promise of protection.

Seventy years ago, this promise and this trust were trampled underfoot.

I would like to recall the words that the [future] chief rabbi of France, Jacob Kaplan, wrote to Marshal Pétain in October 1940, after the introduction of the despicable Statute of the Jews. "As the victims of measures that undermine our human dignity and our honor as Frenchmen, we express our profound faith in the spirit of justice of the Eternal France. We know that the ties uniting us with the great French family are too strong to be broken."

Therein lies the betrayal.

Across time, beyond grief, my presence this morning bears witness to France's determination to protect the memory of her lost children and honor these souls who died but have no graves, whose only tomb is our memory.

That is the purpose of the requirement set by the Republic: that the names of those martyred victims should not fall into oblivion.

We owe the Jewish martyrs of the Vélodrome d'Hiver the truth about what happened seventy years ago.

The truth is that French police—on the basis of the lists

they had themselves drawn up—undertook to arrest the thousands of innocent people trapped on July 16, 1942. And that the French gendarmerie escorted them to the internment camps.

The truth is that no German soldiers—not a single one—were mobilized at any stage of the operation.

The truth is that this crime was committed in France, by France.

To his great credit, President Jacques Chirac recognized this truth, in this very spot on July 16, 1995. "France," he said, "France, country of the Enlightenment and human rights, land of welcome and asylum, France, that day, was committing the irreparable."

But the truth is also that the crime of the Vél d'Hiv was committed against France, against her values, against her principles, against her ideal.

Honor was saved by the Righteous, by all those who were able to rise up against barbarism, by those anonymous heroes who hid a neighbor here, helped another there, and risked their lives to save those of innocent people. By all those French people who enabled three quarters of France's Jews to survive.

France's honor was embodied by General de Gaulle, who stood up on June 18, 1940, to continue the struggle.

France's honor was defended by the Resistance, the shadow army that would not resign itself to shame and defeat.

France was represented on the battlefields, with our flag, by the soldiers of the Free French Forces.

She was also served by the Jewish institutions, like the Oeuvre de secours aux enfants [Children's Welfare

Organization], which secretly organized the rescue of more than five thousand children and took in orphans after the Liberation.

The truth does not divide people. It brings them together. In that spirit, this day of commemoration was established by François Mitterrand, and the Foundation for the Memory of the Shoah was created under Lionel Jospin's government. Set up under that same govern-ment, with Jacques Chirac, was the Commission for the Compensation of Victims of Spoliation Resulting from Anti-Semitic Legislation in Force During the Occupation, whose aim was to put right what still could be put right.

In the chain of our collective history, it now falls to me to continue this common duty of remembrance, truth, and hope.

It begins with passing on the memory. Ignorance is the source of many abuses.

We cannot tolerate the fact that two out of three young French people do not know what the Vél d'Hiv roundup was.

The Republic's schools—in which I hereby voice my confidence—have a mission: to instruct, educate, teach about the past, make it known and understood in all its dimensions. The Holocaust is on the curriculum of the final primary and junior school years and the second *lycée* year.

There must not be a single primary school, junior school, or *lycée* in France where it is not taught. There must not be a single institution where this history is not fully understood, respected, and pondered over. For the Republic, there cannot and will not be any lost memories.

I personally shall see to this.

The challenge is to fight tirelessly against all forms of falsification of history: not only the insult of Holocaust denial, but also the temptation of relativism. Indeed, to pass on the history of the Shoah is to teach how uniquely appalling it was. By its nature, its scale, its methods, and the terrifying precision of its execution, that crime remains an abyss unique in human history. We must constantly remind ourselves of that singularity.

Finally, passing on this memory means preserving all its lessons. It means understanding how the ignominy was possible then, in order that it may never recur in the future.

The Shoah was not created from a vacuum and did not emerge from nowhere. True, it was set in motion by the un-precedented and terrifying combination of single-mindedness in its racist frenzy and industrial rationality in its execution. But it was also made possible by centuries of blindness, stupidity, lies, and hatred. It was preceded by many warning signs, which failed to alert people's consciences.

We must never let our guard down. No nation, no society, nobody is immune from evil. Let us not forget this verdict by Primo Levi on his persecutors. "Save the exceptions, they were not monsters, they had our faces." Let us remain alert, so that we may detect the return of monstrosity under its most harmless guises.

I am aware of the fears expressed by some of you. I want to respond to them.

Conscious of this history, the Republic will pursue all anti-Semitic acts with the utmost determination, but also all remarks that may lead France's Jews even to feel uneasy in their own country.

In this area, nothing is immaterial. Everything will be fought with the last ounce of energy. Being silent about anti-Semitism, dissimulating it, explaining it already means accepting it.

The safety of France's Jews is not just a matter for Jews, it is a matter for all French people, and I intend it to be guaranteed under all circumstances and in all places.

Four months ago, in Toulouse, children died for the same reason as those of the Vél d'Hiv: because they were Jews.

Anti-Semitism is not an opinion, it is an abhorrence. For that reason, it must first of all be faced directly. It must be named and recognized for what it is. Wherever it manifests itself, it will be unmasked and punished.

All ideologies of exclusion, all forms of intolerance, all fanaticism, all xenophobia that seek to develop the mentality of hatred will find their way blocked by the Republic.

Every Saturday morning, in every French synagogue, at the end of the service, the prayer of France's Jews rings out, the prayer they utter for the homeland they love and want to serve. "May France live in happiness and prosperity. May unity and harmony make her strong and great. May she enjoy lasting peace and preserve her spirit of nobility among the nations."

All of France must be worthy of this spirit of nobility.

To tirelessly teach historical truth, to scrupulously ensure respect for the values of the Republic, to constantly recall the demand for religious tolerance, within the frame of our *laïque* [secular] laws never to give way on the principles of freedom and human dignity, always to further the promise of equality and emancipation. Those are the measures we must collectively assign ourselves.

In thinking of the lives never allowed to blossom, of those children deprived of a future, those destinies cut short, we must raise still further the demands we make of our own lives. By refusing indifference, neglect, and complacency, we shall make ourselves stronger together.

It is by being clear-sighted about our own history that France, thanks to the spirit of harmony and unity, will best promote her values, here and throughout the world.

Long live the Republic! Long live France!

About the Author

© Louis Monier

Maurice Rajsfus (b. 1928) is an activist and former investigative journalist for *Le Monde*. He is the author of thirty books, including many examining the Vichy regime and its legacy in French police culture. He has also written about Drancy concentration camp and Israel-Palestine, as well as co-authored several illustrated books about history. In 1990, Rajsfus and several friends founded "Ras l'Front," an anti-Le Pen association of far-left-wing organizations extremely active in the 1990s against the rise of nationalist parties in France and fascist ideas. They worked together and promoted leftist causes through a monthly publication as well as actions. He served as chairman from 1991–1999. From 1994–2012 Rajsfus created and circulated "Que fait la police," a "Cop Watch" bulletin with press clippings detailing human rights abuses by French police. His books about the Vél d'Hiv raid and his experiences during WWII have been brought together to form the basis of a YA comic (Tartamudo editions) as well as a play written and directed by Philippe Ogouz, which was then adapted for film in 2010, *Souvenirs d'un vieil enfant: La rafle du Vel' d'Hiv* (Memories of an Old Child: The Roundup of the Vel' d'Hiv), directed by Alain Guesnier. Maurice Rajsfus lives in Paris with his wife, and has two sons as well as several grandchildren and great-grandchildren.

Contributor Biographies

LEVI LAUB (b. 1938) is an activist and occasional translator who worked with the Progressive Labor Party in the United States for 15 years primarily as an organizer of immigrant labor in the California Valleys. In 1963 Laub led a group of 59 students to Cuba via Prague, violating and challenging the travel ban for U.S. citizens that was in place at the time. Upon his return to the United States, Laub was called before the House Un-American Activities Committee. Riots broke out in the hearing room when Capitol police were called in to remove Laub and his supporters. Within the month, Laub and three other organizers of the Cuba trip were indicted in Federal Court for violating the Travel Ban. In U.S. v. Laub, the Supreme Court ruled in his favor, considering it unconstitutional to disallow American citizens their right to free movement. Laub met Maurice Rajsfus in Paris while doing research into communist militancy in the French Resistance, about which Rajsfus wrote a book entitled *L'an prochain, la revolution* (Next Year, The Revolution).

MICHEL WARSCHAWSKI (b. 1949) (Mikado) is an Israeli anti-Zionist peace activist and journalist. He was born in Strasbourg, France, where his father was a rabbi. He moved to Jerusalem for Talmudic studies at age 16 and later completed a degree in philosophy at the Hebrew University of Jerusalem. He led the Marxist Revolutionary Communist League (Matzpen, Israeli Section of the Fourth International) until its demise in the 1990s, and co-founded the Alternative Information Center (AIC), an organization uniting Israeli and Palestinian anti-Zionist activists. His books include *On the Border* (South End Press) and *Towards an Open Tomb—The Crisis of Israeli Society* (Monthly Review Press).